THE OPEN SECRET

". . . to make the word of God fully known, the mystery hidden from all ages and generations but now made manifest to his saints. To them God chose to make known how great among the nations are the riches of the glory of this mystery, which is Christ in you, the hope of glory."

Colossians 1:25–27

THE OPEN SECRET

Sketches for a Missionary Theology

by

Lesslie Newbigin

WILLIAM B. EERDMANS PUBLISHING COMPANY
GRAND RAPIDS, MICHIGAN

Library of Congress Cataloging in Publication Data

Newbigin, James Edward Lesslie, Bp.
 The open secret.

 Includes index.
 1. Mission of the church. 2. Missions—Theory.
I. Title.
BV601.8.N4 1978   266   78-16423
ISBN 0-8028-1752-1

Grateful acknowledgment is made for permission to quote from the
following sources:

Personal Knowledge by Michael Polanyi, by permission of The University of
Chicago Press. Copyright © 1958 by The University of Chicago Press. Also
by permission of Routledge & Kegan Paul Ltd. Copyright © 1958 by
Routledge & Kegan Paul Ltd.

Theology of Liberation by Gustavo Gutierrez, by permission of Orbis Books.
Copyright © 1972 by Orbis Books.

"The Basis, Purpose and Manner of Interfaith Dialogue," *Scottish Journal
of Theology*, vol. 30, by permission of Scottish Academic Press Ltd.

"Christ and the Cultures," *Scottish Journal of Theology*, vol. 31, by permission of Scottish Academic Press Ltd.

Contents

Preface   vii

1   *The Background of the Discussion*   1
2   *The Question of Authority*   13
3   *The Mission of the Triune God*   20
4   *Proclaiming the Kingdom of the Father: Mission as Faith in Action*   32
5   *Sharing the Life of the Son: Mission as Love in Action*   44
6   *Bearing the Witness of the Spirit: Mission as Hope in Action*   62
7   *The Gospel and World History*   73
8   *Mission as Action for God's Justice*   102
9   *Church Growth, Conversion and Culture*   135
10   *The Gospel among the Religions*   181

2943

Preface

THE MATERIAL here presented has been developed in the course of a four-year period during which I have been privileged to lecture in theology to men and women preparing for missionary service — whether in their own countries or abroad. They come for relatively short periods. They have little time for leisurely academic study. They are facing their life work, and they want to be able to reach as much clarity as possible about the mission on which they are going. These lectures have been given in the hope of helping them to do this.

Those participating in the courses have represented a wide range of academic and practical experience. Many of them have had no previous experience in theology as an academic discipline; some have had a full theological training and considerable experience. They have come from all the six continents and from a wide range of Christian confessions.

I am conscious of the fact that these lectures leave much to be desired from the point of view of the scholar who is aware of the range of contemporary studies — biblical, theological, and missiological. I must ask the reader to remember the purpose for which and the context in which they were prepared.

The original germ of what is here presented was

embodied in a pamphlet entitled "Trinitarian Faith for To-day's Mission" published at the time of the integration of the International Missionary Council with the World Council of Churches. The invitation to teach at the Selly Oak Colleges has provided me with a welcome opportunity to develop these thoughts.

Because this is not a work of academic scholarship I have not attempted to furnish it with an array of footnotes indicating all the sources from which I have learned. It is indeed hardly possible to trace all these, and I must simply make the obvious remark that I am deeply in debt to countless friends and colleagues whose speech and writing have stimulated my own thought. I am especially grateful to Paul Clifford and my other colleagues in the Selly Oak Colleges for their friendship and encouragement.

Part of this material was given as a course at Princeton Theological Seminary in the summer of 1977, and I am most grateful to Dr. McCord for this invitation. I have also a special debt of gratitude to Dr. Arthur Bauer of the Lutheran Church in America who came to these lectures and used his gracious influence to persuade me to write and Mr. Eerdmans to publish the material.

Mr. Eerdmans and his staff have been most diligent and helpful publishers, and I am most grateful for their unfailing help.

Finally I must express deep gratitude to my colleague Miss Verleigh Cant who converted my illegible scribblings with almost flawless accuracy into lucid type, in the course of her already very busy life.

Selly Oak   Lesslie Newbigin
Birmingham, England
June 1978

1

The Background of the Discussion

"CHRIST IS THE LIGHT of the nations." With these majestic words the Second Vatican Council began the greatest of its documents, the "Constitution on the Church." Fundamental to everything else that came forth from the council were the reaffirmation of the missionary character of the church, the recognition of the unfinished task which that implies, the confession that the church is a pilgrim people on its way to the ends of the earth and the end of time, and the acknowledgment of the need for a new openness to the world into which the church is sent.

This new readiness to acknowledge the missionary character of the church, to confess that "there is no participation in Christ without participation in his mission to the world,"[1] is not confined to the Roman Catholic church. All the old established churches of the Western world have been brought to a new recognition that mission belongs to the very being of the church. "Mission," of course, is not a new word, but it is being used in a new way. All the churches of Western Christendom — Catholic and Protestant — have been familiar with missions. But missions were enterprises which belonged to the exterior of church life. They were

---

1. Willingen Conference of the International Missionary Council (1952).

1

carried on somewhere else — in Asia, Africa, or the South Pacific, in the slums of the city, or among the gypsies, the vagrants, the marginal people. In many contexts a "mission church" was the second-class institution in the downtown quarter of the city, in distinction from the well-heeled institution in the affluent quarter which was just "the church." In some forms of the ecclesiastical vernacular, a "missionary diocese" was a diocese which had not yet graduated to the full status of a diocese without qualification. Theological faculties might have provided a place for "missions" as a branch of practical theology, but it had no place in the central teaching of Christian doctrine. To put it briefly, the church approved of "missions" but was not itself the mission.

In the preceding paragraph I have used past tenses. No doubt there are still large parts of Christendom where the present tense would still be applicable. However, most thoughtful Christians in the old, established Western churches can no longer use this kind of language. They recognize that, with the radical secularization of Western culture, the churches are in a missionary situation in what once was Christendom. Moreover, the struggles through which the younger churches born of Western missions have had to pass in order to graduate from "mission" to "church" have forced the older churches to recognize that this separation of church from mission is theologically indefensible. More and more Christians of the old churches have come to recognize that a church which is not "the church in mission" is no church at all. Consequently the agenda papers of church conferences are liberally sprinkled with discussions about the church's mission. For the first time in many centuries the question of the nature of the church's missionary task is a burning issue for debate within the heart of the older churches. Deeply held convictions on the subject clash with each other and — in some places at least — polarization has reached the point where anathemas are in the air. (See, for example, the "Frankfurt Declaration on the Fundamental Basis of Mission," 1970.) This is a new situation, and it is full of promise. The present discussion is written in the hope of placing the debate in a broad biblical perspective and in the hope that to do so will release new energies for the contemporary mission of the church, not only in its global dimensions but also in its application to the tough new paganism of the contemporary Western world.

I

It seems wise to begin the discussion with a glance at the historical background of missions. Any attempt to deal with the present without awareness of what has gone before can only lead to distorted vision and false judgment. At the risk of absurd oversimplification, let me try to sketch the earlier chapters of the story in which we now have to play our part.

The story begins with the vast explosion of love, joy, and hope released into the world by the resurrection from the tomb of the crucified and rejected Jesus. The shock waves of that explosion spread within a few years to all the quarters of the compass. We are familiar with its spread westwards to Rome and so throughout Europe, but characteristically we forget the other parts of the story. From Antioch, the first great missionary center where there were both Greek- and Syrian-speaking Christians, the gospel spread not only westward into the Greek-speaking world, but eastward in its Syrian form along the ancient trade routes linking the Mediterranean with central Asia, India, and China. By the end of the second century Edessa was the capital of a Christian state. By the year 225 there were more than twenty Christian bishops in what is now Iraq. Armenia was a Christian nation by the end of the third century. In 410 the Persian Empire granted recognition to the church in a concordat which established the separate authority of the church over its own members — the system later to be adopted by the Muslims. By the fifth century there were Christian bishops in Meshed, Herat, and Merv, and the gospel had made its way right into the heart of Asia. Many of the Arabian tribes had become Christian as early as the

3

second century. The gospel had come to India — possibly with the coming of Thomas himself. Ethiopia had accepted the gospel by the middle of the fourth century.

It was into the midst of this Eastern Christendom, so largely forgotten by the Western church, that Islam was born. Another mighty explosion formed the half-Christian tribes of Arabia into a warrior nation and carried the power of Islam within a century of the Prophet's death right through the old heartland of Christendom, subduing the mighty Persian Empire, Syria, Egypt, and the whole southern shore of the Mediterranean. From there it was not long before the armies of Islam had conquered Spain, southern France, Sicily, and southern Italy and had marched right up to Rome itself, where the bishop was forced to pay tribute to the Muslim power.

Meanwhile, the pagan tribes from the north were ravaging the whole of northern and western Europe, wiping out the Christian culture so wonderfully developed in the preceding centuries. An observer living towards the end of the ninth century could have been forgiven for thinking Christianity was a lost cause. In the vast areas held by Islam, Christians had become second-class citizens enclosed within the confines of the Millet system and precluded from any active evangelism. And the Western Church itself had become something of a large ghetto, dominated and largely surrounded by the superior culture and military power of Islam.

It is important for a right understanding of the issue with which this book is concerned to remember that a great deal of the substance of the Western Christian tradition — its liturgy, theology, and church order — was formed during the long period in which Western Christendom was an almost enclosed ghetto precluded from missionary advance. Church and people were one society struggling to maintain itself against a superior power. There was little possibility that the church could see itself as a society sent out in mission to all peoples.

The movement by which Western Christendom began to

gather strength to reassert itself against the power of Islam has interesting parallels with the recent history of national movements among the colonies of the Western powers. Historians of the Indian national movement (to take only one example) agree that it was the injection of European ideas through the educational system that fueled the beginnings of nationalism. In a similar way the revival of Western Christendom after the Dark Ages was greatly indebted to the infusion of new thought through the translation into Latin from early in the twelfth century of the Arabic thought which had been developed by the synthesis of Greek science and philosophy with Islamic theology. (For this gift Western Christendom remains permanently indebted to Islam and — beyond that — to the Nestorian and other Eastern Christians who were the teachers of Greek learning to the semibarbarian peoples from Arabia in the early centuries of Islam.)

The long struggle of Western Christendom to break out of the Muslim grip had its focus in the Iberian peninsula. When after centuries of struggle the Iberian peoples achieved their liberation, they were the pioneers in daring voyages of exploration designed to circumvent the Muslim power, break its grip on the trade with the East, and find a way to the sources of the spices of East Asia, without which Europe could not live.

Islam was a theocratic system in which there was a fusion of religious faith and political power even more complete than was the case in the Christian society. The counterattack against Islam was likewise an enterprise in which religious faith, political and military power, and commercial enterprise were inextricably mixed. Spanish and Portuguese penetration into Asia and the Americas made little distinction between political and ecclesiastical control. When the northern European powers — Danish, British, and Dutch — joined in the game, the emphasis was perhaps more on its commercial aspect, but the essential character of the enterprise was the same. Asia, the Americas, and — later — Africa experienced the impact of Western missions

5

as an integral part of a whole movement in which the military, political, commercial, cultural, and religious aspects were inextricably blended. In this respect the global expansion of Western power was neither new nor strange. It was one more example of a constantly repeated human experience. It has been, perhaps, the most far-reaching in history. It looms large in our view because it is the most recent of its kind. It is too near us to be seen in its true proportions or to be evaluated in all its mixture of good and evil. The one thing that can certainly be said about this chapter of human history is that it is over. For more than two centuries it has provided the framework in which the Western churches have understood their world missionary task. To continue to think in the familiar terms is now folly. We are forced to do something that the Western churches have never had to do since the days of their own birth — to discover the form and substance of a missionary church in terms which are valid in a world which has rejected the power and the influence of the Western nations. Missions will no longer work along the stream of expanding Western power. They have to learn to go against the stream. And in this situation we shall find that the New Testament speaks to us much more directly than does the nineteenth century as we learn afresh what it means to bear witness to the gospel from a position not of strength but of weakness.

The reader will rightly recognize that I am indulging in very sweeping historical generalizations. The picture is much more complicated when one begins to look at the detail. To look only at the most recent chapter of the story shows that the rejection of Western leadership by the rest of the world has developed through various stages and is not yet complete. A century ago the Western nations so dominated the world that most of the rest of mankind stood in awe of the white man and accepted his claim to political, cultural, and religious leadership. Even when the movements for political emancipation began, the leaders of national movements accepted in large measure the cultural leadership of the West, using Western languages, political ideas, and forms of organization. A second stage can be observed (for example, in the movements which have ousted Congress from power in India) in which these are rejected and recourse is had to native languages and cultures and to more ancient traditions of social life. But even with this there is still a general readiness to accept the science and technology of the West because of the tangible benefits which they seem to bring. It is not clear that this will continue to be so. The West is coming to realize the fearful human cost of its science and technology and cannot assume that it will continue to enjoy forever the almost universal authority which is now accorded to them. We have lived through two decades in which "development" was held out as the goal to which all efforts should be directed, and development was understood as movement by the peoples of the third world in the direction taken by the peoples of Europe and North America. We are now emerging from this period. It can no longer be assumed that this is the goal. We must expect that the rest of the world will raise yet more radical questions about the goal which the developed world has taken for granted since the period of the Enlightenment, and which still governs most of our thinking.

One almost universal feature of the world scene, however, seems unlikely to change in the near future. It is what has been described as the revolution of rising expectations. People in every part of the world are agreed in making demands upon society which in former ages were made only by a small segment in each nation. The French and American revolutions opened a radically new chapter in human history by establishing governments committed to the restructuring of human life on the principles developed during the Enlightenment. These principles were embodied in a popular and explosive form in Thomas Paine's "The Rights of Man." They were experienced in revolutionary movements through the nineteenth century and achieved apocalyptic expression in the Marxist vision of a new world

to emerge from Armageddon — a world in which every
man's need would be met by the willing contribution of each
according to his ability. The driving force of this vision
extends far beyond its Marxist expression. It is emodied in
the "Four Freedoms" of F. D. Roosevelt and in the promises
which any political party must now make if it is to have a
hope of power. It is indeed true that there are still millions
of men and women patiently tilling the fields of Asia as their
ancestors did with no expectation that life will ever be
otherwise than it has always been — a life of almost cease-
less labor, of recurrent hunger, and of very drastically limited freedom. But the movement is inexorably towards the
rejection of this agelong bondage. Everywhere men demand
and governments promise "the right to life, liberty, and the
pursuit of happiness," and everywhere men grow impatient
and rebellious when the promise is not fulfilled; if there is
one generalization about the human situation today which is
almost universally valid, it is surely this. The inner relationship between this expectation of a new world and the
Christian gospel of the reign of God is one of the issues
which must be discussed in any contemporary theology of
mission.

One more key fact in the new situation of the Christian
world mission remains to be stated. It is, of course, that the
church now exists as a global fellowship present in almost
every part of the world and is increasingly conscious of its
universal character. This "great new fact of our time," as
William Temple called it, is the fruit of the missionary work
of the past three centuries. Whatever criticisms we may
have to make of that work, nothing can take away from our
sense of wonder and thanksgiving as we contemplate this
new fact. All thinking about the world mission of the church
today must thankfully and joyfully take account of the fact
that the "home base" of missions is now nothing less than
the worldwide community, and every proposed expression
of the church's missionary outreach must be tested by asking whether it can be accepted by the whole ecumenical
family as an authentic expression of the gospel.

II

In what ways and with what degree of success have the Western churches adjusted their thinking about missions to meet the new realities? Once more I must take the risk of trying to answer this question with a few sweeping generalizations in order to provide the perspective for the discussion which follows.

The World Missionary Conference of 1910 was already thinking in truly global terms and was aware of the deeply evil elements in the impact of Western power on the peoples of Asia, Africa, and the Pacific. But the younger churches were only marginally acknowledged, and there was a still unshaken confidence in the future of Western civilization as the bearer of the gospel to the "backward peoples." At Jerusalem in 1928 there was a fuller acknowledgment of the younger churches and a much more acute awareness of the ambiguities of Western power and of the worldwide impact of Western secularism. At Tambaram ten years later there was a new awareness of the worldwide church as the people entrusted with the gospel and called to do battle with a paganism which was showing its power in the heart of the old Christendom.

In the years following the Second World War, the church-centered concept of mission was further consolidated. At Willingen (1952) there was a strong affirmation of mission as central and essential to the life of the whole church seen as a world fellowship, but in the course of that meeting a new insistence began to be felt upon the need for a missiology which was not domesticated in the church. The 1960 conference, convened at Strasbourg by the World's Student Christian Federation on "The Life and Mission of the Church," saw the emergence of a radically secular interpretation of the *missio Dei*. The assembled students were challenged "to move out of the traditional Church structure in open, flexible and mobile groups" and "to begin radically to de-sacralise the Church."[2] In the following decade the

---

2. *The Student World* 54, nos. 1–2 (1961), pp. 81–82.

concept of mission in those circles influenced by the ecumenical movement was strongly influenced by this radically secular vision. Mission was primarily concerned with the doing of God's justice in the world, not primarily with increasing the membership of the church. In the influential book of Arendt van Leeuwen, *Christianity and World History*, the process of secularization was hailed as the present form of the impact of the biblical message upon the traditional societies. The World Council of Churches' study of missionary structures for the congregation affirmed that it is the world, not the church, which "writes the agenda."[3] And at Uppsala in 1968 the Fourth Assembly of the WCC accepted a definition of mission which identified it primarily with action for humanization in the secular life of the world. The traditional concept of "mission fields," identified as geographical areas lying beyond the frontiers of Christendom, was replaced by the concept of "priority situations for mission," identified as situations where, irrespective of the presence or absence of the church, action for human dignity was called for.

Concurrent with these developments, and to some extent related to them, was the development of a new attitude toward the world religions. This called for a relationship of dialogue and (where appropriate) partnership to replace traditional attitudes often stigmatized as "proselytizing." With a recognition of the secular as the sphere of God's action in history came the call to recognize also his action within the world religions.

A vehement attack on these developments was launched in 1970 by the "Frankfurt Declaration on the Fundamental Crisis of Missions," mainly the work of Peter Beyerhaus of Tübingen. Less polemical, but probably more influential, was the "Wheaton Declaration" of 1966, adopted at a conference called by conservative evangelical missionary agencies in the United States claiming to represent the work of more than 11,000 overseas missionaries. This declaration,

---

3. *The Church for Others*, pp. 20–23.

while rejecting the missiological developments in the World Council of Churches, sounded also the call to take seriously and penitently into account the issues of unity and social justice which were motivating missionary thinking in the WCC. The ensuing decade saw meetings at Bangkok (1977), Lausanne (1974), and Nairobi (1975) which showed that on both sides of this debate there is a serious intention to listen to what the other side is saying. The Nairobi report on "Confessing Christ Today" is a particularly valuable attempt to state a call to mission which is "holistic" in taking with full seriousness both the call to personal conversion and the call to action for God's justice in the world. This statement has already done much to lift the debate above the level of mutually destructive polemics.

But the debate must continue. It is to a large extent not a debate between different bodies but a debate within each of the churches. The ensuing discussion will show, I hope, that it is a debate that leads into the deepest questions of faith. I do not want to trivialize it by using cheap slogans. But in this preliminary sketch I must run the risk in order to bring out one important point. The internal polarization within each of the churches is rendered more damaging by the fact that it is often embodied in a structural dichotomy. The concern of those who see mission primarily in terms of action for God's justice is embodied mainly in programs carried on at a supracongregational level by boards and committees, whether denominational or ecumenical. The concern of those who see mission primarily in terms of personal conversion is expressed mainly at the level of congregational life. The effect of this is that each is robbed of its proper character by its separation from the other. Christian programs for justice and compassion are severed from their proper roots in the liturgical and sacramental life of the congregation, and so lose their character as signs of the presence of Christ and risk becoming mere crusades fueled by a moralism which can become self-righteous. And the life of the worshiping congregation, severed from its proper expression in compassionate service to the secular community around it, risks becoming a self-centered existence serving only the needs and desires of its members. Thus both sides of the dichotomy find good reasons for caricaturing each other, and mutual distrust deepens.

I believe, however, that our first need is for theological understanding and that the reordering of structures must follow this. In the following pages I want to suggest a framework within which we can develop a style of living and speaking which will do justice to the truth in the different convictions which are so often in mutually destructive conflict.

2

The Question of Authority

I HAVE ALREADY suggested that one of the important factors in the present situation is that the Western peoples, who have been responsible for the major part of the missionary outreach of the past three centuries, are no longer accepted as leaders by the rest of the world. When one reads the missionary literature of fifty years ago one is struck by the calm assurance of the superiority of the white man's culture, the confidence that it was only a matter of time before the whole world would receive its blessings, and the unconscious identification of the gospel with the good elements in that culture. In this atmosphere even the vehement rejection of the gospel — for example, by Muslims and by the higher castes of Hinduism — could not easily shake the assurance of the missionary and the church which sent him.

Today the situation is different. The question "What right do you have to preach to us?" is one that is asked with a confidence and a vehemence unusual fifty years ago. To this question it is useless to answer by quoting the Great Commission or other texts of Scripture. Why should a Hindu accept the authority of the Christian Scriptures? It is useless to point to the achievements of Christianity in human history; the record is too ambiguous for that. Nor is it enough to speak of being constrained by love, for what has

13

to be shown is that it is truly a work of love to call men and women out of their traditional allegiances, and to invite them to accept — with all the cost involved — the yoke of obedience to Christ.

Indeed, it is not only the adherents of other faiths who press the question. From within the Christian church voices are raised to question the whole enterprise of missions, if missions are understood to involve calling people of other faiths to conversion. It is easy to identify these questions.

Why not join with the sincere adherents of all religions in seeking the fullness of the truth to which they all aspire?

Why not join with all people of goodwill in tackling the real human problems of hunger, oppression, sickness, and alienation, instead of seeking more adherents for your religious group?

Is your enterprise not an offense against the unity of mankind? Is not the just unity of all peoples a matter of such urgency that to propagate something so divisive as religion is almost a crime against humanity? In the presence of such tragedies as we witness in Northern Ireland and Lebanon, what right have you to engage in a program which is more likely to promote division than unity?

The first step in responding to these questions is to ask the counterquestion which uncovers the hidden assumptions behind the question. What grounds have you for thinking you will come nearer to a solution of the world's problems by combining the insights of all the religions? What makes you think it is religion that provides the clue to man's real needs?

What is your program for tackling the problems of poverty and oppression? Are you not the victim of illusion if you imagine that a program for creating economic justice on a world scale will unite mankind? Is it not precisely in the conflict of ideologies which use words like "justice" and "freedom" as their slogans that the most murderous conflicts are generated?

What is your program for the unity of mankind? Around

what center and in what organized form do you propose to unite mankind? If you can produce your program I can tell you whether it is less likely or more likely than the enterprise of Christian missions to promote division.

The point of the counterquestions is that they force us to recognize that the questions themselves imply certain commitments about the way in which the whole human situation can be understood and in which we can seek to respond to it. The Christian mission rests upon one such commitment. It is in fact the practical working out of that commitment. It is futile to try to establish its validity by appealing to some other commitment — that is, by claiming that it ministers to human unity, to development, or to liberation. This must be said sharply at the present moment in view of the uncritical way in which missions in the last three decades have been promoted in terms of their contribution to world development. I shall have much to say later about the necessary involvement of missions in world development, but only after I have affirmed my belief about the nature of the authority of the mission. The question of authority is not to be answered by trying to demonstrate the usefulness of missions for some purpose which can be accepted apart from the ultimate commitment upon which the missionary enterprise rests.

The question of authority was raised at the very outset of the mission, in the ministry of Jesus himself. Men noted that he spoke "as one who had authority," but there was something perplexing about the authority, for it was "not as their scribes" (Matt. 7:29). The authority of the scribes was a derived authority. It consisted in their knowledge of and ability to handle the primary authority — that of the revealed Torah. The authority of Jesus was of a different kind: he spoke as one who himself had authority. What was this authority? During the tense week of the passion the question was put to him directly: "By what authority are you doing these things, or who gave you this authority to do them?" (Mark 11:28). The questioners were seeking something that would either link Jesus with an authority they

15

already recognized or discredit him by showing that there was no such link. The questions could not be answered in the terms they were seeking. The authority of Jesus is not a derived authority; it is the authority of God himself present in the life of men. So Jesus puts the counterquestion which will test their capacity to recognize that authority: "Was the baptism of John from heaven or from men?" The baptism of John was that event which marked "the beginning of the gospel" (Mark 1:1-4) because it was the event in which Jesus recognized the call of his Father. The scribes are unable to recognize this authority because it would involve a commitment incompatible with the commitments they have made. Their question therefore cannot be answered. Because the authority of Jesus is ultimate, the recognition of it involves a commitment that replaces all other commitments.

In the same way the apostles at the beginning of their mission are challenged with the question, "By what power, or by what name did you do this?" The only possible answer is, "In the name of Jesus" (Acts 4:7-10). They can only refer to "the name of Jesus," and by that name they refer to an ultimate authority and to their own final commitment to that authority. The authority of Jesus cannot be validated by reference to some other authority which is already accepted. The naming of his name calls for nothing less than a fresh and radical decision about one's ultimate commitment.

To meet the question "By what authority?" with the answer "In the name of Jesus" is obviously to invite the counterquestion, "Who is Jesus?" The answering of that question is the work of Christian witness through all the centuries and all the cultures until the day comes when all nations confess him Lord. In the following chapters we shall be concerned with the beginnings of the answer. Very specially we shall be looking at the reasons for which the simple formula "In the name of Jesus" had to be expanded into the formula "In the name of the Father, Son, and Holy Spirit." But some further reflections will be in order regarding my answer to the question "By what authority?"

16

The Question of Authority

1. My answer to this question is a personal commitment. I am — in Pascal's famous phrase — wagering my life on the faith that Jesus is the ultimate authority. My answer is a confession: I believe. It is a personal commitment to a faith which cannot be demonstrated on grounds established from the point of view of another commitment. In saying "I believe" in this way, the Christian is placing himself in a position like that of the scientist who affirms his belief in the truth of a statement in physics. All statements which claim to speak the truth about realities external to the speaker are affirmations of faith to which the speaker commits himself. These statements are not passively received in the mind of the speaker, like the reproduction of a picture on a photographic film by the light from an external object falling on it. Instead, they are the results of the continuing effort of the community of scientists seeking to grasp more fully the meaning of all the objects perceived by means of larger and larger generalizations about their mutual relations. They are the fruit of a continuing and passionate endeavor in which the scientific community is sustained by a faith in the validity of its methods. The Christian commitment is distinguished in that it is a commitment to a belief about the meaning of the whole of human experience in its entirety — namely, the belief that this meaning is to be found in the person of Jesus Christ, incarnate, crucified, risen, and destined to reign over all things. I make this commitment as part of and in dependence on the community of those who have lived by this faith from its beginning. The mission in which I participate is the continuing action of this community in living out this faith in wider and wider areas of experience.

2. The confession I am making is that Jesus is the supreme authority or, using the language of the New Testament, that "Jesus is Lord." This confession implies a claim regarding the entire public life of mankind and the whole created world. It is a claim that by following the clue which is given in the story which constitutes the gospel, the believing community will be led to a true understanding of all

17

that is and to a right practical relation to it. Like the claim of the scientist with respect to his discoveries, it is a claim that the truth of what is believed will be confirmed in new discoveries which cannot be specified in advance. The community which confesses that Jesus is Lord has thus been, from the very beginning, a movement launched into the public life of mankind. The Graeco-Roman world in which the New Testament was written was full of societies offering to those who wished to join a way of personal salvation through religious teaching and practice. There were several commonly used Greek words for such societies.[1] At no time did the church use any of these names for itself. It was not, and could not be, a society offering personal salvation for those who cared to avail themselves of its teaching and practice. It was from the beginning a movement claiming the allegiance of all peoples, and it used for itself with almost total consistency the name *ecclesia* — the assembly of all citizens called to deal with the public affairs of the city. The distinctive thing about this assembly was that it was called by a more august authority than the town clerk: it was the *ecclesia Theou*, the assembly called by God, and therefore requiring the attendance of all. The church could have escaped persecution by the Roman Empire if it had been content to be treated as a *cultus privatus* — one of the many forms of personal religion. But it was not. Its affirmation that "Jesus is Lord" implied a public, universal claim that was bound eventually to clash with the *cultus publicus* of the empire. The confession "Jesus is Lord" implies a commitment to make good that confession in relation to the whole life of the world — its philosophy, its culture, and its politics no less than the personal lives of its people.

The Christian mission is thus the acting out in the whole life of the whole world of the confession that Jesus is Lord of all.

3. One more point has to be made, and it is essential. I would be distorting the truth if I simply spoke of this con-

---

1. See K. L. Schmidt in *Theological Dictionary of the New Testament*, ed. G. Kittel (Grand Rapids: Eerdmans, 1965), vol. 3, pp. 501–536.

fession as being mine alone. I make this confession only because I have been laid hold of by Another and commissioned to do so. It is not primarily or essentially my decision. By ways which are mysterious to me, which I can only faintly trace, I have been laid hold of by one greater than I and led into a place where I must make this confession and where I find no way of making sense of my own life or of the life of the world except through being an obedient disciple of Jesus. I have therefore to say with Paul: "Necessity is laid upon me. Woe to me if I do not preach the gospel. For if I do this of my own will, I have a reward; but if not of my own will, I am entrusted with a commission" (I Cor. 9:16–17). The origin of my confession is not in me. It is committed to me. I am simply the messenger entrusted with the responsibility to deliver the message. "You did not choose me," says Jesus to his apostles, "I chose you and appointed you that you should go and bear fruit" (John 15:16).

The mission is God's, not ours. But God chooses men and women for the service of his mission. To be a Christian is to be part of the chosen company — chosen, not for privilege, but for responsibility. The doctrine of election, so central to the whole of the Bible, is necessarily central for a true understanding of missions. It has been misconstrued and therefore widely rejected. The rejection of false and immoral forms of the doctrine of election is right. But no doctrine of the Christian mission can be true which does not recognize that it is God's sending, and that he sends whom he will.

3

The Mission of the Triune God

TO THE QUESTION of authority the first answer is, as we have seen, "in the name of Jesus." It is by this name that Paul introduces himself in his letters: he is a messenger sent by Jesus, called and sent by one greater than himself. There is no authority beyond that to which he can appeal. But that answer necessarily prompts the next question. Who is Jesus? How is that question to be answered? The first and most natural answer finds its model in the first answer to Jesus' question, "Who do men say that I am?" He is "one of the prophets." This, as Jesus suggests, is the natural answer of "flesh and blood" (Matt. 16:17). For the Hindu he is one of the *jeevanmuktas* who have attained in this life the full realization of the divine. For the Muslim he is one of the messengers of Allah. For the man of modern Western society he is one of the world religious leaders to whom one will find reference (along with Buddha, Muhammed, Moses, and Guru Nanak) in the "Religion" section of *Time Magazine* but not in the section on "World Affairs." He is one of an acknowledged class. His introduction does not disturb the structure of ideas of which this classification is a facet.

This, as I have said, is the "natural" answer. As a first step it is unavoidable. As a missionary in India I often shared in evangelistic preaching in villages where the name

"Jesus" had no more meaning than any other strange name. I have heard speakers use many different Tamil words to explain who he is. He is *Swamy* ("Lord"). Or he is *Satguru* ("the true teacher"). He is *Avatar* ("incarnation of God"). Or he is *Kadavul* ("the transcendent God") who has become man. What all these words have in common is that they necessarily place Jesus within a world of ideas which is formed by the Hindu tradition and which is embodied in the language of the people. *Swamy* is usually translated "Lord," but it does not have the meaning that the word *Kurios* had for a Greek-speaking Jew. It denotes not Yahweh, the Lord of the Old Testament, but one of the myriad gods who fill the pages of the Hindu epics. *Avatar* is usually translated "incarnation," but there have been many *avatars* and there will be many more. To announce a new *avatar* is not to announce any radical change in the nature of things. Even to use the word *kadavul* will only provoke the question, if Jesus is *kadavul*, who is the one to whom he prays?

The example which I have taken from personal experience is simply a reminder of the fact that one cannot begin to answer the question "Who is Jesus?" without using a language — and therefore a structure of thought — which is shaped by the pre-Christian experience of the one who asks the question. There is no way of avoiding this necessity. And yet the introduction of the name of Jesus placed the structure under a strain which it cannot bear without breaking. Jesus is now not just Lord, but unique Lord, not just *avatar*, but unique *avatar*. The word *kadavul* can no longer refer to a monad: it must refer to a reality, within which there is a relationship of hearing and answering.

The event by which the old structure is broken is not a natural happening. Jesus tells Peter that the confession "You are the Christ, the Son of the Living God" is not the work of "flesh and blood" but a gift of the Father (Matt. 16:17). It is not a human achievement but a gift from above. It is the primary work of the Spirit of God himself (I Cor. 12:1-3; I John 4:1-3). It is the action of God by which he chooses and anoints the messengers of his reign. It

21

is the work of the sovereign Spirit to enable men and women in new situations and in new cultural forms to find the ways in which the confession of Jesus as Lord may be made in the language of their own culture. The mission of the church is in fact the church's obedient participation in that action of the Spirit by which the confession of Jesus as Lord becomes the authentic confession of ever new peoples, each in its own tongue.

But how do we begin to say who Jesus is? As the first generation of Christians moved out of the culture of Judaism into the cosmopolitan culture of the Graeco-Roman world it had to develop a way of doing this. The way it developed is embodied in the new style of literature of which Mark's Gospel is our earliest exemplar. Here a story is told in such a way as to provide, not a biography in the modern style, but an answer to the question, Who is Jesus?

> The beginning of the gospel of Jesus Christ, the Son of God. As it is written in Isaiah the Prophet,
> "Behold, I send my messenger before thy face, who shall prepare thy way; the voice of one crying in the wilderness: Prepare the way of the Lord, make his paths straight —"
> John the baptizer appeared in the wilderness, preaching a baptism of repentance for the forgiveness of sins. And there went out to him all the country of Judea, and all the people of Jerusalem; and they were baptized by him in the river Jordan, confessing their sins. Now John was clothed with camel's hair, and had a leather girdle around his waist, and ate locusts and wild honey. And he preached, saying, "After me comes he who is mightier than I, the thong of whose sandals I am not worthy to stoop down and untie. I have baptized you with water; but he will baptize you with the Holy Spirit."
>
> In those days Jesus came from Nazareth of Galilee and was baptized by John in the Jordan. And when he came up out of the water, immediately he saw the heavens opened and the Spirit descending upon him like a dove; and a voice came from heaven, "Thou art my beloved Son; with thee I am well pleased."
>
> The Spirit immediately drove him out into the wilderness. And he was in the wilderness forty days, tempted by Satan; and he was with the wild beasts; and the angels ministered to him.

Now after John was arrested, Jesus came into Galilee, preaching the gospel of God, and saying, "The time is fulfilled, and the kingdom of God is at hand; repent, and believe in the gospel." (Mark 1:1-15)

In this brief introductory paragraph Jesus is introduced as the one who announces the coming of the reign of God, the one who is acknowledged as the Son of God and is anointed by the Spirit of God.

1. He announces the reign of God. God was known already in Israel as one who reigns. He had made known his sovereignty in delivering Israel out of the slavery of Egypt. He was indeed sovereign over all the earth, though the nations did not know it. In age after age Israel had been summoned to "say among the nations" that "the Lord reigns" (Ps. 96:10). Through centuries of crushing defeat and humiliation a remnant in Israel had kept alive the faith that the sovereign Lord would in the end reveal his hidden kingship, tear aside the illusions behind which evil carries on its work, dethrone the idols, and come to reign in justice over the nations.

Jesus announces that that day has dawned. But the announcement is also a call to a radical reversal of normal attitudes. Israel has been eagerly awaiting the coming of the Lord's rule but looking for it in the wrong direction. The announcement is therefore at the same time a call to turn around and look the other way — to repent. Only as part of such a radical turnabout can Israel receive the gift of faith — faith to believe that the reign of God is indeed present, faith to know the secret of the kingdom of God (Acts 4:11). This secret is the "good news" which the church publishes, the "gospel."

Jesus is thus not the initiator or founder of the kingdom. It is God's kingdom. Jesus is the one who is sent as herald and bearer of the kingdom.

2. Jesus is acknowledged as the Son of God. The most characteristic word on the lips of Jesus seems to have been the Aramaic word *Abba*, a word used as the most informal

23

and intimate mode of speech from a son to his father. It was not, apparently, a word that was ever used in prayer to God. But it seems to have been so much the characteristic way in which Jesus prayed that it was carried over into the language of the Greek-speaking church. Paul can speak of it as the sign of our sonship given to us by the Spirit (Rom. 8:12–17). Jesus' characteristic use of this word points to the deepest secret of his being. He was "the Son." In the fourth Gospel this is very specially emphasized and we are told that the glory which his disciples saw in him was "glory as of the only Son from the Father" (John 1:14). Though Jesus is the bearer of the kingdom, he is yet at the same time the obedient Son. The sovereignty which he brings and which puts to flight the demonic powers (Mark 1:27) is not exercised in his own name but in the name of the Father. It is exercised by one who looks up in loving obedience as a son to a father.

3. Jesus is anointed by the Spirit. In the Old Testament the Spirit is the living active power of God, giving life to all and empowering men to perform special service or to receive special revelation. It is the "breath of the Lord," and the life and power of the Lord are in it. In many passages of the Old Testament the promise is made that the Spirit of the Lord will rest upon the one whom he sends to be the agent of his justice. The voice which Jesus heard at his baptism echoes the words of Isaiah 42:1: "Behold my servant, whom I uphold, my chosen, in whom my soul delights; I have put my spirit upon him, he will bring forth justice to the nations." And according to Luke's Gospel Jesus interprets the words of Isaiah 61:1–2 as foreshadowing his ministry. "The Spirit of the Lord God is upon me, because the Lord has anointed me to bring good tidings to the afflicted, he has sent me to bind up the brokenhearted, to proclaim liberty to the captives, and the opening of the prison to those who are bound; to proclaim the year of the Lord's favor" (Luke 4:18–19).

The acknowledgment of Jesus as Son and his anointing by the Spirit took place, according to the record, at his baptism by John in the Jordan, the event which is described as "the beginning of the gospel." John's baptism seems to have been a symbolic action in the tradition of the prophets of Israel. Jeremiah had smashed an earthenware pot as a vivid and unforgettable sign of God's impending judgment on Jerusalem, and Isaiah had gone naked and barefoot as a sign of the coming calamities in Egypt and Ethiopia. Other examples can be cited. The message of John was one of impending judgment; God was coming to purge his people with fire, to cut down the barren trees (Matt. 3:10; cf. Isa. 5), and to sift the wheat from the chaff (Matt. 3:12). John called people to repentance in order that they might escape the coming judgment. The baptism in the Jordan was a symbolic action which affirmed the call to a radical new beginning for Israel, and the acceptance of baptism was a symbol that the call had been heard and accepted. But it was only a symbol. The real thing, when it came, would not be water but a devouring fire, the very breath of the Lord (Mark 1:8; cf. Luke 3:16–17).

Jesus was one of those who heard and accepted the call. His first appearance in the story was as one of a crowd of unnamed men and women who had been convicted of sin and had heard and accepted the call to repentance. As one of them Jesus was baptized. He took his place as part of sinful humanity. And in that action he received the anointing of the Spirit. At the same moment the word of God spoken through Isaiah sounded in his ears. He is the beloved Son, anointed by the Spirit to bring forth justice to the nations.

The baptism in the Jordan was only a beginning. It had to be completed by a crowded ministry in which Jesus acted out his identification with sin-burdened humanity (Matt. 8:17). It had to be consummated on Calvary, where his baptism was complete (Luke 12:50; Mark 10:38). And that consummation of his baptism opened the way for the whole company of his chosen apostles to receive the same anointing of the Spirit, to be acknowledged as children of God, and to be sent out to bring God's justice to the nations.

Here, then, is the first answer to the question, "Who is Jesus?" He is the Son, sent by the Father and anointed by the Spirit to be the bearer of God's kingdom to the nations. This is the Jesus who was proclaimed by the first Christians to the world of their time.

Any missionary, in fact anyone engaged in the business of communication, knows very well that what is spoken and what is heard are by no means always the same. What is heard is necessarily shaped by the thought-world of the hearer. What was it that was heard when the story about Jesus was spoken into the thought-world of the Roman Empire of the first two centuries?

To attempt to describe that thought-world in a few paragraphs would be absurd. But what can be said, simply and truthfully, is that it was a world controlled by presuppositions radically different from those which governed the thought-world of the Judaism of which Jesus was a part. Fundamental among these presuppositions was that the really real, the ultimate source of all being, must be beyond and above the ordinary world which we see and hear, taste and handle. It must be beyond time, for time implies change and change implies imperfection. It must be beyond space, for space is the arena of our sense experience, which can never give us absolute truth. No particular event in history, therefore, can be more than an illustration or symbol of the timeless, changeless, passionless, purely spiritual entity which is ultimate being.

This meant that all thinking was controlled by certain inescapable dichotomies. In science there was the dichotomy between the intelligible world and the sensible world, between that which can be known of pure being by the rational and spiritual powers of the mind and that which can be experienced through the five senses, which can never give access to being itself. In history there was the dichotomy between virtue and fortune. The world of external happenings is not under the undisputed control of pure reason. It is the sphere either of the purely irrational, or of fate. Man's history is the story of the conflict between this and whatever equipment of intelligence, skill, and courage he can bring to the conflict.

Within such a world view there is room for, and in fact necessity for, a whole range of intermediate entities to bridge the gap between the pure being which is essentially unknowable and unapproachable and the ordinary world of things and events. As in the similar thought world of India, it was natural to place Jesus somewhere in this intermediate range. Jesus, an actual man with a place in history, could not be identified with the One who is beyond all change and all multiplicity. That would be simple nonsense. But the very name "Son" implies subordination, and therefore Jesus could be understood either as some kind of emanation from the One, or even as among the first of creatures. Or else he could be understood as a man who had been brought into an exceptionally or even uniquely close relationship with the One — in Indian terms, a *jeevanmukta*. The story of the first three centuries of the Christian era furnishes a rich variety of variations on these themes. What they have in common is that they leave intact the classical thought world. They leave unhealed its dichotomies. Above all they leave it with a God finally uninvolved in human history.

Against this the mind of the church fought a long, stubborn, often confused but finally successful battle. It did so because at the very heart of its life, its thought, and its worship was the figure of the one who had died on the cross and had been raised from the dead — "the Son of God," as Paul says, "who loved me and gave himself up for me." There is a famous graffito in Rome which depicts a man lifting up his hands in worship before a figure with an ass's head stretched out on a cross. Underneath is written "Anexamenos worships his god." Presumably some pagan slave was mocking his Christian fellow slave. The picture vividly suggests both the stubborn strength of the Christians' insistence on the deity of Christ, and the horror and contempt which this aroused in that classical world. The absolutely crucial point was this: in the man Jesus God had actually suffered for the sin of the world. For that assurance

Christians were ready to go to the lions. If it was true, the whole classical world view was false and had to be replaced by something radically different.

In his book *Christianity and Classical Culture* C. N. Cochrane tells the story of the development of classical thought from its brilliant restoration under Augustus to its disintegration in the fifth century. By that time a new way of understanding the whole human situation had been developed, and it was the work of Augustine to build on this foundation the beginnings of the new world view that would shape the thought of Western Christendom for a thousand years. This new way of understanding was embodied in the doctrine of the Trinity. As we have seen, this doctrine is already implicit in our earliest written answer to the question, "Who is Jesus?" — implicit but not yet fully thought out. It was the work of the great theologians of the first three centuries, especially of Athanasius, to develop this implicit understanding into a model which would replace the classical axioms with a new set of axioms. The ultimate reality, according to this new view, is not to be understood as a timeless, passionless monad beyond all human knowing, but as a trinity of Father, Son, and Spirit. This understanding is not the result of speculative thought. It has been given by revelation in the actual historical life and work of the Son.

Accepted thus by faith it becomes the starting point for a new way of understanding the world. It cannot be understood and much less can it be verified by reference to the assumed axioms of classical thought. It is verified only by the action of the Holy Spirit present in the witness of the martyrs. But accepted by faith it becomes the basis of a new way of making sense of the world, not just by speculative science, but by practical wisdom.

Thus, on this new basis the dichotomy between the sensible and the intelligible worlds is healed, for God himself has actually been made flesh. The Son who offered the perfect sacrifice of loving obedience to the Father on the cross is not the Father, but he is truly God as the Father is

God. The being of God himself is involved in the suffering of history. And through the Spirit the Christian can share this suffering, knowing that in doing so he is in touch with the very being of God himself (Rom. 8:18–27). Likewise the dichotomy between virtue and fortune is healed, for the Christian who thus shares in the travail of history also knows that God works everything for good to those who love him (Rom. 8:28). His life here in the midst of history is thus not a hopeless battle against fate, but the faithful following of Jesus along the way of the cross in loving obedience to the Father whose rule is over all. A wholly new way is opened up to accomplish what classical science and philosophy could not accomplish — a way of grasping and dealing with the reality of human life as part of a meaningful history within a world created and sustained by the God who had revealed himself in Jesus and who continued by his Spirit to guide the followers of Jesus into the fullness of the truth.

The language in which this trinitarian faith was wrought out was necessarily the language of that time and place. The crucial word upon which the central conflict turned was the word *homoousios*, a word which expressed in the language of contemporary philosophy the conviction that the being of the Son and the being of the Spirit are the very being of the Godhead and are not something intermediate between a remote and ultimately unapproachable Supreme Being and the known world of nature and history. On the firm maintenance of that conviction everything depended. In that sense the church can never go back on what was then decided. But it is also true that it is not enough for the church to go on repeating in different cultural situations the same words and phrases. New ways have to be found of stating the essential trinitarian faith, and for this the church in each new cultural situation has to go back to the original biblical sources of this faith in order to lay hold on it afresh and to state it afresh in contemporary terms.

It has been said that the question of the Trinity is the one theological question that has been really settled. It would, I

29

think, be nearer to the truth to say that the Nicene formula has been so devoutly hallowed that it is effectively put out of circulation. It has been treated like the talent which was buried for safekeeping rather than risked in the commerce of discussion. The church continues to repeat the trinitarian formula but — unless I am greatly mistaken — the ordinary Christian in the Western world who hears or reads the word "God" does not immediately and inevitably think of the Triune Being — Father, Son, and Spirit. He thinks of a supreme monad. Not many preachers, I suspect, look forward eagerly to Trinity Sunday. The working concept of God for most ordinary Christians is — if one may venture a bold guess — shaped more by the combination of Greek philosophy and Islamic theology which was powerfully injected into the thought of Christendom at the beginning of the High Middle Ages than by the thought of the fathers of the first four centuries.

If, as I have argued, we are forced to answer the question of authority by the words "In the name of Jesus"; and if we then have to answer the question, "Who is Jesus?", we shall only be able to answer that question in terms which embody the trinitarian faith. Like the earliest Christians we shall have to expand our first answer so that it runs, "In the name of the Father, the Son, and the Holy Spirit." And this means that, like them, we shall be offering a model for understanding human life — a model which cannot be verified by reference to the axioms of our culture but which is offered on the authority of revelation and with the claim that it does provide the possibility of a practical wisdom to grasp and deal with human life as it really is.

I have been encouraged to think that this is a fruitful approach to the subject of this book by reading the parallel which Michael Polanyi has drawn between our time and the time for which Augustine wrote. At the crucial turning point of his great book, *Personal Knowledge*, Polanyi writes:

> The critical movement, which seems to be nearing the end of its course today, was perhaps the most fruitful effort ever sustained by the human mind. The past four or five centuries, which have gradually destroyed or overshadowed the whole

medieval cosmos, have enriched us mentally and morally to an extent unrivalled by any period of similar duration. But its incandescence had fed on the combustion of the Christian heritage in the oxygen of Greek rationalism, and when this fuel was exhausted the critical framework itself burnt away.

Modern man is unprecedented; yet we must now go back to St. Augustine to restore the balance of our cognitive powers. In the fourth century A.D., St. Augustine brought the history of Greek philosophy to a close by inaugurating for the first time a post-critical philosophy. He taught that all knowledge was a gift of grace, for which we must strive under the guidance of antecedent belief: *nisi credideritis, non intelligitis.*[1]

Polanyi's plea is for a "post-critical philosophy" without which he believes science must destroy itself. In developing his reference to Augustine, Polanyi insists that "the process of examining any topic is both an exploration of the topic, and an exegesis of our fundamental beliefs in the light of which we approach it; a dialectical combination of exploration and exegesis. Our fundamental beliefs are continuously reconsidered in the course of such a process, but only within the scope of their own basic premises."[2]

The Christian mission, as I understand it, has an analogous logical structure. It is an acting out of a fundamental belief and, at the same time, a process in which this belief is being constantly reconsidered in the light of the experience of acting it out in every sector of human affairs and in dialogue with every other pattern of thought by which men and women seek to make sense of their lives.

The fundamental belief is embodied in the affirmation that God has revealed himself as Father, Son, and Spirit. I shall therefore begin by looking at the Christian mission in three ways — as the proclaiming of the kingdom of the Father, as sharing the life of the Son, and as bearing the witness of the Spirit. From this I shall go on to look at contemporary issues in mission from the point of view of this trinitarian faith.

---

1. Michael Polanyi, *Personal Knowledge* (Chicago: Univ. of Chicago Press, 1958), p. 265.

2. Ibid., p. 267.

4

Proclaiming the Kingdom of the Father: Mission as Faith in Action

WE BEGIN with what Mark calls "the beginning of the gospel." Jesus came into Galilee "announcing the good news of God and saying, 'The time is fulfilled, the reign of God is at hand; repent and believe the good news'" (Mark 1:14–15).

The announcement concerns the reign of God — God who is the creator, upholder, and consummator of all that is. We are not talking about one sector of human affairs, one aspect of human life, one strand out of the whole fabric of world history; we are talking about the reign and about the sovereignty of God over all that is, and therefore we are talking about the origin, meaning, and end of the universe and of all man's history within the history of the universe. We are not dealing with a local and temporary disturbance in the current of cosmic happenings, but with the source and goal of the cosmos. That is why it was inevitable that the answering of the question, "Who is Jesus?" forced the writers of the New Testament further and further back. As a missionary trying to introduce the name of Jesus to those who do not know it, I have always been perplexed by the question of where to begin. Mark begins with the baptism of

John; Matthew, with Abraham; and Luke, with Adam. But the writer of the prologue to the fourth Gospel is compelled to press still further back and to introduce Jesus as the one who was with God and was God from the beginning, the Word through whom all things were made.

The Bible is unique among the sacred books of the world's religions in that it is in structure a history of the cosmos. It claims to show us the shape, the structure, the origin, and the goal, not merely of human history, but of cosmic history. It does not accept a view of nature as simply the arena upon which the drama of human history is played out. Much less does it seek the secret of man's true being within the self — a self for which the public history of the world can have no ultimate significance. Rather it sees the history of the nations and the history of nature within the large framework of God's history — the carrying forward to its completion of the gracious purpose which has its source in the love of the Father for the Son in the unity of the Spirit. The first announcement of the good news that the reign of God is at hand can only be understood in the context of this biblical sketch of a universal history. The reign of God is his reign over all things.

But if the Bible is in form a universal history, it is at once clear that it has a very special structure. All history is written by a process of selection and omission. What is deemed to be significant for the story as a whole is selected, and the rest is omitted. But the principle of selection in the Bible is clearly different from that employed by a modern historian. Although the perspective is cosmic and universal, at each stage the story proceeds by a process of narrowing. The broad picture is replaced at each stage by a close-up focused on one part of the whole.

Thus, to begin with the Genesis story of man's second start after the disasters of total corruption and the flood, the saga shows us Noah and his family coming out of the ark and receiving the unconditional promise of God's blessing on his whole race and on the physical world. Mankind sets out under the rainbow arch which is the sacrament of the pri-

33

mal covenant with all mankind and with the created world
for man's sake. He is told to be fruitful and multiply and to
replenish the earth. Immediately there follows the list of
the seventy nations, "the heathen," who are the fruit of the
blessing. These "nations" will be in the background of the
story which follows, but at the outset we are reminded that
their existence is the fruit of God's primal blessing
(Gen. 10).

There follows the sad story of the effort of the nations to
create their own unity. It is the archetype of all imperial
adventures, for "imperialism" is the name we give to programs for human unity other than those initiated by ourselves. Its name is Babel — archetype of megalopolis, of
Nineveh and of Rome. Its end is disaster and estrangement.

Patiently God makes yet another new beginning. Among
the seventy nations the camera focuses on the family of Eber
(Gen. 10:25). Among the descendants of Eber, Abraham is
chosen to begin the adventure of faith, to go out from his
own people, not knowing the end of the road but trusting the
one who calls. He is promised the blessing, but it is not only
for himself: it is for the nations. He will be the bearer of
God's primal promise of blessing for all the nations.

But the narrowing continues. Not all of Abraham's children are chosen to be the bearers of the blessing; Isaac is
chosen, Ishmael is not. Among Isaac's sons Jacob, not Esau,
is chosen. As the story goes on the narrowing continues.
Among the tribes of Israel, Judah is chosen and the rest
disappear to the margin of the picture. And within Judah it
is only a smaller and smaller remnant that is the bearer of
the blessing.

But the rest never disappear wholly from the picture.
Those who are chosen to be bearers of a blessing are chosen
for the sake of *all*. The covenant of Noah is not revoked. The
promised blessing is, in the end, for all the nations.
Abraham, Israel, the tribe of Judah, and the faithful remnant are the chosen bearers of it.

Bearers — not exclusive beneficiaries. There lay the
constant temptation. Again and again it had to be said that

election is for responsibility, not for privilege. Again and again unfaithful Israel had to be threatened with punishment *because* she was the elect of God. "You only have I known of all the families of the earth; *therefore* I will punish you for all your iniquities" (Amos 3:2 — my italics). The meaning of Israel's election and of her misunderstanding of it is depicted with supreme dramatic power in the story of Jonah, which is perhaps the most moving interpretation of the missionary calling of God's people to be found in the Bible. Jonah (Israel, God's chosen people) is called to go and bear witness in the midst of Nineveh (Babylon, Rome, the pagan world with all its awesome power and wealth). Jonah cannot face the challenge. He seeks to evade it and escape from the pressure of God's calling. He thinks he has succeeded. He sleeps soundly (the church somnolent) while God whips up a raging storm and the pagan sailors devoutly pray for deliverance. It is the pagans who have to summon Jonah to his prayers. When lots are cast Jonah is forced to confess his guilt. But he also confesses his God — "the God of heaven who made the sea and the dry land." Jonah is ready to pay for his sin with his life, but the conversion of the pagan sailors by this improbable missionary has already begun. They labor to save Jonah and they pray to the Lord. But Jonah must be thrown to the sea. The corn of wheat must fall into the ground and die. The elect must suffer. The church must lose its life.

But out of death there is a resurrection. A penitent and restored Jonah goes to speak God's word to the pagan world, and his obedience is met by a stupendous miracle. There is universal repentance. The pagan world has been humbled. But Jonah is utterly disappointed. The heathen are not to be punished after all. What justice can there be in a world where God is so absurdly generous (cf. Matt. 20:1–16)? What is the point of missions if hell is going to be unnecessary? Jonah is frustrated and angry. He settles himself on the edge of the city (was it — as a Tamil Christian friend of mine has suggested — the mission compound?) "to see what would become of the city." And we are left with the picture of Jonah sulking while God pleads with him for Nineveh, that great city with its thousands of innocent babies and its dumb animals — God so tenderly pleading for the pagan world and Jonah so sullenly wrapped up in his own self-pity.

It is Jonah who must take God's message to Nineveh. He is the elect bearer of God's promise of blessing for the nations. No one else can bring the blessing. But the election and the promise are for Nineveh, for the nations, not for Jonah alone. As God's chosen one he must suffer. God will not let him off. But God will also not let him go. For God does not cancel his calling.

If a footnote to the story is allowed, we may take it from another story of a storm at sea recorded in Acts 27. From the point of view of the story of salvation, it is Paul who is at the centre of the story's interest. The rest of the ship's company scarcely interests us. It is Paul who must carry the word of God to Rome. Yet at the height of the storm God says to Paul: "Do not be afraid, Paul; you must stand before Caesar; and, lo, God has granted you all those who sail with you" (Acts 27:24). God's purpose of blessing has its focus, at the moment, on Paul; but its scope includes all who travel with him.[1]

The Bible, then, is concerned with God's purpose of blessing for all the nations. It is concerned with the completion of God's purpose in the creation of the world and of man within the world. It is not — to put it crudely — concerned with offering a way of escape for the redeemed soul out of history, but with the action of God to bring history to its true end. The Old Testament therefore is full of visions of a restored humanity living in peace and happiness within a renewed creation. These visions are not of an otherworldly bliss, but of earthly happiness and prosperity (Pss. 72 and 144), of wise and just government, of a renewed nature in which kindness has replaced the law of the jungle (Isa. 11:1–9).

---

1. I owe the thought to a sermon preached by D. T. Niles.

But this universal purpose of blessing is not to be effected by means of a universal revelation to all humanity. There is, as we have seen, a process of selection: a few are chosen to be the bearers of the purpose; they are chosen, not for themselves, but the sake of all. The inner logic of this pattern of election — the few on behalf of the many — will be discussed in Chapter 7. Meanwhile we follow the story through the Old Testament with its repeated narrowing of the focus to a smaller and smaller remnant until we reach the moment which is "the beginning of the gospel," the moment when the focus is narrowed down to one who bears the whole purpose of cosmic salvation in his own person and who is hailed as the beloved Son in whom the Father is well pleased. He, the beloved Son, the chosen one, comes forth to announce that the long-awaited reign of God is at hand.

What does the proclamation mean? The reign of God is not a new "movement" in which those interested may enlist. It is not a cause calling for support, a cause which might succeed or fail according to the amount of support it attracts. It is, precisely, the reign of God, the fact that God whom Jesus knows as Father is the sovereign ruler of all peoples and all things. The announcement means that this fact is no longer something remote — far up in the heavens or far away in the future. It is an impending reality, in fact, the one great reality which confronts men and women now with the need for decision.

But in what way has the coming of Jesus brought the reign of God near? What is the relation of Jesus to the reign? Is it that he now, as God's anointed, takes control of world events and shapes them to God's will? Does he become the master and manager of the world's affairs on behalf of God? Certainly the "powers of the kingdom" are manifest in him. He does mighty works which to eyes of faith are signs of the presence of the reign of God (Luke 11:14–22). Yet, paradoxically, his calling is to the way of suffering, rejection, and death — to the way of the cross. He bears witness to the presence of the reign of God, not by overpowering the forces of evil, but by taking their full weight upon himself. Yet it is in that seeming defeat that victory is won.

Consequently, the reign of God is a reality which can only be announced in parables. It is a "mystery," at once both hidden and revealed. The characteristic language in which Jesus proclaims the kingdom is the language of parable. When asked to explain this he quotes the terrible words with which Isaiah received his commission as a prophet: "Go and say to this people: 'Hear and hear, but do not understand; see and see, but do not perceive'. Make the heart of this people fat, and their ears heavy, and shut their eyes; lest they see with their eyes, and hear with their ears, and understand with their hearts, and turn and be healed" (Isa. 6:9–10). Jesus tells his disciples that the secret of the kingdom has been given to them but that to others it will be riddles so that the hardening of the heart of which Isaiah spoke will happen. The principle of election is still at work. A few are called to be bearers of the secret of God's purpose. The announcement of the kingdom will *not* of itself open men's eyes to its presence, for the reign of God is present under the form, not of power, but of weakness. It is strictly a mystery, a reality which remains hidden unless it is revealed by the action of God.

Not only do the words of Jesus have this character of parable, but his works also have the same character. They are signs of the kingdom only to those to whom eyes of faith are given. When John the Baptist sends to ask, "Are you the Coming One or not?", Jesus replies by referring to his deeds of power in language which recalls the prophetic words of Isaiah 35, and he adds: "Blessed is he who takes no offense at me" (Luke 7:23). The mighty works of Jesus do not *necessarily* manifest the presence of the reign of God. They have the same two-edged character the parables have. They can cause those who hear of them to stumble, or for some — and blessed are these — they can be the occasion of faith.

The supreme parable, the supreme deed by which the reign of God is both revealed and hidden, is the cross. When Israel rejected Jesus' call to repent and believe the good news of the reign of God, there were two roads which (humanly speaking) he might have taken. One would have been to withdraw with his disciples to the desert and there, like the contemporary communities of which we know from the Qumran documents, pray and wait for God's action to establish his reign. The other would have been to take the way of the contemporary "freedom fighters" and seek to establish the messianic order by force. Jesus did neither. He led his disciples right into the Holy City at the season dedicated to the memory of national liberation. He chose a mount, however, that suggested a humble royalty, a kingly meekness. He challenged the leaders of the nation at the very center of their power, and he accepted in his self the full onslaught of the powers that refuse the reign of God. Here is the supreme parable: the reign of God hidden and manifest in the dying of a condemned and excommunicated man; the fullness of God's blessing bestowed in the accursed death of the cross. Who could believe this unless it was given to him by an act of God's sovereign grace? To know the power and the wisdom of God in the weakness and foolishness of the cross is not an achievement of ordinary human discernment. It is not the work of "flesh and blood." It is the gift of God to those who are called to receive it (I Cor. 1:24). That the cross is indeed victory and not defeat is made manifest in the resurrection of Jesus from the dead. The resurrection is not the reversal of a defeat but the manifestation of a victory. And this manifestation was "not to all the people" but to those "who were chosen by God as witnesses" (Acts 10:41). It is not true, though it is often said, that the risen Jesus manifested himself only to believers. Saul of Tarsus was not a believer. What is true, and it is in line with the consistent teaching of the New Testament, is that the risen Jesus was manifested to those whom God chose — not for themselves, but to be witnesses to all.

The resurrection is, however, more than "the manifestation of a victory." It *is* this, but it is more. It is the "firstfruits" (I Cor. 15:23) of a harvest which is still to come and which is the end of all God's works, the putting of all things into subjection to God's reign. This is the consistent interpretation of the resurrection both in the Epistles and in the Gospels. The manifestations of the risen Christ to his apostles are not only demonstrations of the fact that he is risen; they are also the occasion for pointing the apostles forward towards a task and a promise that lie in the future. They are the assurance that victory has been won and that therefore all nations and all things must be claimed for him who has conquered. The initial announcement of the "good news," namely, that "the reign of God has drawn near," is validated by the resurrection. But the content of the announcement is still a mystery entrusted to a few in order to be communicated to all. The reign of God is both revealed and hidden in the words and works of Jesus and supremely in his cross and resurrection. It has to be proclaimed to all the nations by those to whom its secret has been entrusted.

Let me summarize what has been said up to this point in answer to the question, "In what way has Jesus brought the reign of God near?" Negatively I have said it has not been done by the introduction into history of a power which is manifest to the natural perception of men and women and which will therefore progressively overcome and eliminate the powers which oppose it. Positively I have said that the coming of Jesus has introduced into history an event in which the reign of God is made under the form of weakness and foolishness to those to whom God has chosen to make it known, and that it is made known to them so it may be proclaimed to all. Because it is the reign of God that is proclaimed, it is the true secret of universal and cosmic history. It is not a program for private deliverance but is the hidden reality by which the public history of mankind is to be understood. The seals that close the scroll of history so that it is hidden from natural human perception have been broken by the slain Lamb who is the Lion of the tribe of Judah (Rev. 5:1–10). Therefore he, and he alone, can and does reveal its meaning to those whom he chooses. As they follow the Lamb on the way he went, they bear witness to the true meaning of what is happening in the history of the world.

One of the most popular slogans in the missiology of the past two decades is "God is at work in the world." It is, in one sense, indisputable. What can and must be disputed is that the apparently successful movements and forces are the work of God. This rests on a view of human affairs which has not taken adequate account of sin. But what also cannot be disputed is that we are required to read "the signs of the times" and to interpret them truly so that we may know how to act rightly. Proclaiming the reign of God over all events and things must involve some kind of interpretation of what is happening in the world, however provisional, modest, and tentative it may be. Unfortunately the history of Christian attempts to discern the signs of the times makes discouraging reading. At many times and places Christians have been sure that the line of God's action was clearly discernible in the growth and influence of the church, in movements of social and political change. These judgments have often been the occasion of shame and embarrassment for Christians of the next generation.

Does the New Testament help us to understand the shape of public events in the light of the proclamation of the kingdom by Jesus? As far as I can see, the answer to this question is to be sought in the so-called apocalypses of the New Testament — the "Little Apocalypse" of Mark 13 and its parallels, and the great Apocalypse which forms the last book of our Bible.

What these apocalyptic passages do is to sketch for us the public history of the world in a form which is shaped by the cross and resurrection of Jesus. Parallel to the repeated assertion that the Son of Man *must* suffer is the assertion regarding the tribulation of history that "these things *must* take place" (Mark 13:7). The form of the cross is projected across the picture of world history. It is not to be a smooth story of successful struggle leading directly to victory. Rather it is a story of tribulation and faithful witness, of death and resurrection.

First there is the warning of false messiahs (Mark 13:5-6). For untold ages people have accepted their

41

lot as something which cannot be radically changed and have accepted the ancient picture of human affairs as part of the cycle of nature, rising only to fall again, being born only to grow old and die. When the idea of total salvation enters into history this cycle is broken. Men begin to dream dreams of a world from which pain, suffering, and injustice have been banished. The vision is created of a single world history leading to a single goal. Politics become messianic. Where the gospel is preached the way is opened for movements offering the hope of total liberation. It is not an accident that in those parts of Asia where Christian penetration has been most thorough, Marxist messianism has also taken root. "Wars and rumors of wars" will be the evidence that the birth pangs of a new age have begun (13:7-8). The world itself will experience the messianic tribulations as a new world struggles to be born. Very specially the church will share these tribulations (13:9). But this very suffering will be the occasion of the Spirit's witness, and this witness must be given to all the nations (13:10-13; cf. John 15:18 and 16:7-15).

The scenario leads on into a still more dreadful crisis where evil enthrones itself in the very city of holiness (Mark 13:14-23), and through the dissolution of the natural order itself (13:24-31) will come the final triumph of God, which will be an act of pure sovereign power and grace. In his own time and in his own way God will fulfill his purpose. Therefore, those to whom the secret has been disclosed must be ready and watchful, faithful to the commission they have received (13:32-37).

It is, no doubt, impossible to say how much, if any, of this passage comes from Jesus himself. In any case its detail reflects the kind of apocalyptic teaching current in some quarters in the time of Jesus and his first disciples. What is important, however, is that we have here an interpretation of coming history which projects forward the proclamation of the kingdom which was the substance of Jesus' message. God's reign is indeed at hand. God is indeed active in history. But his action is hidden within what seems to be its opposite — suffering and tribulation for his people. The secret has been entrusted to those whom God chose. They are to be witnesses of it to all the nations. In fact it will be the Spirit himself who bears this witness in and through the messianic tribulations to which they are called. Their task is to remain faithful to the end. By faith they know that the reign of God has conquered the powers of evil. Their calling is to proclaim that fact to all the nations. They will themselves proclaim it, but even more powerful will be the proclamation of the Spirit, who takes their faithful enduring of rejection as the occasion of his witness.

Mission, seen from this angle, is faith in action. It is the acting out by proclamation and by endurance, through all the events of history, of the faith that the kingdom of God has drawn near. It is the acting out of the central prayer which Jesus taught his disciples to use: "Father, hallowed by thy name, thy kingdom come; thy will be done on earth as in heaven."

5

Sharing the Life of the Son: Mission as Love in Action

JESUS PROCLAIMED the reign of God and sent out his disciples to do the same. But that is not all. His mission was not only a matter of words, and neither is ours. If the New Testament spoke only of the proclamation of the kingdom there could be nothing to justify the adjective "new." The prophets and John the Baptist also proclaimed the kingdom. What is new is that in Jesus the kingdom is present. That is why the first generation of Christian preachers used a different language from the language of Jesus: he spoke about the kingdom, they spoke about Jesus. They were bound to make this shift of language if they were to be faithful to the facts. It was not only that the phrase "kingdom of God" in the ears of a pagan Greek would be almost meaningless, having none of the deep reverberations that it evoked for the man nourished on the Old Testament. It was that the kingdom, or kingship, of God was no longer a distant hope or a faceless concept. It had now a name and a face — the name and face of the man from Nazareth. In the New Testament we are dealing not just with the proclamation of the kingdom but also with the presence of the kingdom.

44

I

At this point we have to pause to take note of the familiar fact that for nearly two centuries there have been scholars who maintain that the shift of language marks a rift in thought; that the "real" Jesus was the one who talked about the kingdom and that the "other" Jesus, who was himself the presence of the kingdom, was a creation of the early church, a myth modeled on contemporary pagan speculation, a product of the untutored piety which, not having been trained in the methods of nineteen-century science, was incapable of distinguishing between facts and fables. On this view the fourth Gospel is regarded as conveying a portrait of Jesus which is almost wholly the product of this untutored piety. The lineaments of the "real" Jesus are to be deciphered only in the first three, and can be traced here only if the reader is alert and watchful to eliminate all intrusive matter from the imagination of the "primitive community."

Much might be said, if this were the occasion, about the unstated presuppositions which underlie many of the critical judgments about what could and could not have been said by Jesus. It is not difficult to show that in many cases these judgments rest upon unexamined assumptions about the nature of God and man which do not arise from the gospel itself. A little research will disclose the hidden credo. That is not my point here. My point is that if it is true that the mission of Jesus was not only to proclaim the kingdom of God but also to embody the presence of the kingdom of God in his own person, then it is understandable that the switch from a Judaic to a Greek environment should have entailed a switch from proclaiming the kingdom to proclaiming Jesus.

Does the evidence warrant the statement that Jesus "embodied in his own person the presence of the kingdom?" Let us exclude, for the present, the evidence of the fourth Gospel and look only at the Synoptics.

When John the Baptist sends messengers to ask: "Are you he who is to come, or shall we look for another?", Jesus answers with a catena of sayings drawn from Isaiah 35:5-6 and 61:1-2, both of which are descriptions of the coming day when Yahweh will personally intervene for salvation and judgment. And Jesus adds to these words of Scripture the warning: "Blessed is he who takes no offense at me" (Matt. 11:6). The day of the Lord is a day both of salvation and of judgment. In the presence of Jesus that day is present, and therefore the warning also must be given. It is in the personal presence of Jesus himself that both the outpouring of salvation and the possibility of "stumbling" are present.

The same passage from Isaiah 61 is quoted by Jesus in the synagogue at Nazareth, followed immediately by the words, "Today this scripture has been fulfilled in your hearing" (Luke 4:21). But here also we learn immediately that the presence of the promised salvation is also the occasion for "stumbling." Jesus is rejected and cast out of the city.

A central feature of the expected day of salvation was the promise that God would forgive the sin of his people. Jesus embodied the fulfillment of that promise in his person. To the paralytic in the house at Capernaum he says, "Son, your sins are forgiven" (Matt. 9:2). This is not the harmless intoning of a familiar cliché; it is an act of awesome authority which immediately provokes the charge of blasphemy. The coming day of the Lord is present — for blessing and for stumbling.

Jesus' conviviality was in obvious contrast with the asceticism of John and provoked the predictable criticism (Matt. 9:14). The reply of Jesus implies that the wedding celebrations have already begun. The feast that the prophets promised has started; it is not the time for fasting. The kingdom is here.

When Jesus sends out the disciples (Matt. 10) they are commissioned to announce the presence of the kingdom and to perform the works which authenticate its presence. At the same time they are authorized to communicate the judgment that comes with the kingdom by shaking off from their feet the dust of any unbelieving town or household. In their coming as his messengers the kingdom itself is present for blessing and for judgment.

So complete is the identification of the presence of Jesus with the presence of the kingdom that a man's acknowledgment or denial of Jesus settles the question of his acceptance or rejection by God. "Everyone who acknowledges me before men, I also will acknowledge before my Father who is in heaven; but whoever denies me before men, I will also deny before my Father who is in heaven" (Matt. 10:32–33). Once again the reality of the reign of God is effectively present in Jesus in its double character of blessing and judgment.

And those who are sent in Jesus' name are also the bearers of that presence, for "he who receives you receives me, and he who receives me receives him who sent me" (Matt. 10:40). This typically "Johannine" phrase (John 13:20) prepares us for the famous passage which has been such an embarrassment to those who would drive a wedge between John and the Synoptics.

> At that time Jesus declared, "I thank thee, Father, Lord of heaven and earth, that thou hast hidden these things from the wise and understanding and revealed them to babes; yea, Father, for such was thy gracious will. All things have been delivered to me by my Father; and no one knows the Son except the Father, and no one knows the Father except the Son and any one to whom the Son chooses to reveal him. Come to me, all who labor and are heavy laden, and I will give you rest. Take my yoke upon you, and learn from me; for I am gentle and lowly in heart, and you will find rest for your souls. For my yoke is easy, and my burden is light. (Matt. 11:25–30)

Joachim Jeremias has given powerful reasons for affirming (on grounds of language, style, and structure) that this saying comes from a Semitic-speaking milieu and for excluding the possibility of regarding it as a "Johannine" saying imported into Matthew's Gospel.[1] Here Jesus in his own per-

---

1. Joachim Jeremias, *New Testament Theology* (London: SCM Press, 1971), I, 57.

son invites all who will to share in the blessings of the reign of God because he is the one to whom its secret has been entrusted. If, as seems reasonable, one accepts this and similar sayings quoted as authentic recollections of the words of Jesus, one has a clue to the later developments which make Jesus, rather than the kingdom, the center of the Christian message. The unwillingness of some scholars to believe that Jesus actually spoke such words appears to rest upon dogmatic rather than upon historical or literary grounds.

Continuing to use only the Synoptic material one could refer to the passages in the Sermon on the Mount where Jesus handles the teaching of the Torah in a way which implies an authority equal to that of the author of the Torah. He does not use the language of the prophets, "Thus says the Lord," but the language of unique authority, "You have heard that it was said [in the law], . . . but I say to you" (Matt. 5:21–48). One could refer also to the words at the end of the Sermon which assume that Jesus will be the judge on the last day and that obedience or disobedience to his words will decide a man's final destiny.

One could continue to illustrate with other examples the fact, which I find impossible to doubt, that Jesus not only spoke about the reign of God, but that in his own mission and ministry the reign of God was obviously present — in other words, that the "Day of the Lord" to which prophets and psalmists had looked forward, the day of Yahweh's decisive intervention for blessing and judgment, had dawned with his coming. I believe that not only was this so, but that Jesus knew it to be so, and that the writer of the fourth Gospel, though he uses his own language to convey the message of Jesus, was not misrepresenting the "Jesus of history" when he portrayed him as one who knew that he was the one "sent from the Father." It is Luke who gives us the deeply significant words of Jesus, speaking to a disciple, with which I must close this part of the evidence: "Blessed are the eyes which see what you see. For I tell you that many prophets and kings desired to see what you see, and did not see it, and to hear what you hear, and did not hear it" (Luke 10:23–24). The longed-for kingdom is not only proclaimed: it is present. But at this point we have to raise a new and vitally important question: Does this presence of the kingdom end with the end of Jesus' earthly ministry? After the removal of Jesus from the reach of sight and sound and touch, are we back again with John the Baptist and the prophets? Is the reign of God once again only something to be proclaimed and prayed for? Or is the presence of the kingdom in Jesus continued through history? What, if anything, do we learn of the intention of Jesus in this matter from the records?

It is notorious that references to the church as a body to continue the ministry of Jesus after his death are very sparsely scattered through the Gospels and are of very questionable value. It is also commonly said that because Jesus expected the immediate advent of the end, therefore a continuing institution cannot have been, and was not, part of his intention. There is a very large literature directed to this question, and I can do no more than state in a summary way what I believe about it, in order to open the discussion of this aspect of missionary theology.

1. It is beyond question that Jesus saw the final consummation of God's purpose of blessing and judgment as an imminent, pressing, immediate reality, something which called for decisive action now and which gave no room for procrastination or indecision.

2. The earliest documents of the New Testament (earlier than the Gospels) show us a church already in being with an ordered and continuous life, a church which understands itself as having Jesus Christ as its foundation (I Cor. 3:11), which practices baptism "into the death of Jesus" (Rom. 6:3), and which regularly shares a meal which is understood as a participation in the body and blood of Christ (I Cor. 10:16). I cannot find in these early letters any trace of the idea that the existence of this church is the result of an improvisation undertaken to repair the breach made by the collapse of the original expectation.

49

3. The popular opinion that the existence of the church as an institution continuing through history is a contradiction of Jesus' vision of the immediacy of the end rests upon a failure to grasp the central point of the Christian view of the "last things." To the discussion of this we shall have to come later. It is essential to a true theology of mission. At this stage it is perhaps enough to put this point sharply as follows. Paul expresses the mind of the earliest Christian community when he speaks of us "upon whom the ends of the ages have come" (I Cor. 10:11). But the Christian believer of today also knows himself to be in the same situation. For him, too, it is the last days. Though he is separated from the early church by nineteen centuries, he is also united with that church in the continuing life of the body of Christ.

4. In seeking to answer the question about Jesus' intention for the period which should follow his death, we must look to one of the most ancient and impregnable elements in the tradition of his words and deeds that has come down to us. It is part of the tradition which Paul received and which he delivered to the churches he founded within twenty years of Jesus' death,

> that the Lord Jesus on the night when he was betrayed took bread, and when he had given thanks, he broke it, and said, "This is my body which is for you. Do this in remembrance of me." In the same way also the cup, after supper, saying, "This cup is the new covenant in my blood. Do this, as often as you drink it, in remembrance of me." For as often as you eat this bread and drink the cup, you proclaim the Lord's death until he comes. (I Cor. 11:23–26)

While there is debate about the precise wording of these sayings, there can be none about the substantial authenticity of the tradition. Here is a piece of hard evidence. It shows Jesus looking towards the future of this community of his disciples. They are to continue to break bread together as they have done so often with him and with the sinners and rejects whom he welcomes into his company. But now these common meals will have a new meaning. He is to be

50

parted from them. They for their part are eager to stay with him, even if it means death. But they cannot do so. What is to be done can be done only by him alone. Nevertheless they are to be his partners in it — afterwards. The bread which they break will be his body given for them. The cup which they share will be his blood shed for them. Their repeated sharing in this common meal will be a continually renewed participation in his dying and, therefore, in his victorious life. At the point of separation, when they are still far from beginning to understand what "the reign of God" means (Luke 22:24), Jesus does a deed and gives a command which will bind them to him in a continually renewed and deepened participation in the mystery of his own being. His life, his cruel death, his resurrection will not only be a story to be proclaimed, recorded, studied: they will be something to be lived. The disciples will thus become themselves part of the revealed secret of the presence of the kingdom. They will be those who, in Paul's words, are "always carrying in the body the death of Jesus, so that the life of Jesus may also be manifested in our bodies" (II Cor. 4:10).

The fourth Gospel does not repeat this account of the words spoken at the supper which is given, with some variations, in the first three. In its place we have the long discourses (John 13–16) which lead up to the great prayer in which Jesus, in consecrating himself to the Father, consecrates his disciples to be sent out into the world to continue his mission. These discourses give a sketch of the way that lies before the disciples as they go out to represent Jesus in the world. They are to be servants one of another just as Jesus has served them (13:1–20). They are to show whose they are by their love of one another (13:34–35). They will find abiding places which the Father provides for them on the way, and they know the way — Jesus himself (13:36–14:11). His going to the Father will open the way for a much more vast ministry which will be marked from their side by love and obedience and from the Father's side by the gift of the Spirit, his abiding presence, and his peace (14:12–31). Through this mutual abiding they will bring forth fruit

51

(15:1-17). The world will hate them, but the hatred of the world will be the occasion for the witness of the Spirit (15:18-27). The Spirit will in fact go before them to convict the world and to guide them into the fullness of the truth (16:8-15). They will share in the travail of the world's new birth, but they will have peace in him (16:16-33). And so these men, to whom Jesus has made the Father fully known (17:1-8) and whom he has guarded from evil (17:9-14), are to be launched into the life of the world as the continuance of his mission and in the power of his consecration (17:15-19). In fact, the glory of God, the glory which tabernacled in the midst of Israel in the wilderness and which dwelt in Jesus (John 1:14), will dwell with the disciples so that the world may recognize in them the sign of the divine mission of Jesus (17:20-23).

There are parallels to the material of these discourses in the Synoptics, especially in the "Little Apocalypse" (Mark 13), which is also concerned with the future mission of the church. But these Johannine discourses are the fullest exposition we have of the intention of Jesus regarding the future of the cause which he entrusted to his disciples and for which he prepared and consecrated them. As I have said, we must assume that the actual wording has been shaped by the evangelist, although from the many echoes (and actual duplicates) of sayings recorded in the Synoptics we can believe that he is not engaging in free composition but is interpreting the intention of Jesus as the memory of it had been preserved and treasured in the church and, very specially, in the memory of the "beloved disciple." Above all the "placing" of these discourses at the point where one would expect the repetition of the words spoken over the bread and the cup, points to the true ground of confidence. This is an exposition of the meaning of the supper, and it is upon the institution of the supper itself that we can most surely ground our certainty about Jesus' intention for the future of his cause. Put briefly, it seems clear that he entrusted the future of his cause to this group of disciples, gave himself completely to them, admitted them into the intimacy of his union with the Father, bound them to himself in the sharing of a meal which, having been part of his shared life with them, would continue after his death, and sent them out to be, not only the teachers of his truth, but the bearers of that glory which he had from his Father. In them the reign of God would not only be proclaimed: it would be present.

5. It is in line with this that the fourth Evangelist gives us his account of the launching of the church upon its mission (John 20:19-23). The words addressed to the Father in the consecration prayer (17:18) are now addressed to the frightened disciples. "As the Father sent me, so I send you" (20:21). He who speaks is recognized by the scars of his passion (20:20). These will be the authentic marks of the body of Christ until the end. His mission is to be their mission. And so also his Spirit is to be theirs (20:22). The Spirit had anointed Jesus for his mission at his baptism in the Jordan. But that was only the beginning. It had to be completed when, on Calvary, he was made completely one with the sin of the world. The cross was the fulfillment of his baptism. Until then we hear nothing of a gift of the Spirit to the disciples. In the Synoptics, even when the twelve are sent out on their mission and given authority to preach and to heal, there is no mention of the Spirit. And John is quite explicit that during the days of Jesus' earthly ministry "the Spirit was not yet given because Jesus was not yet glorified" (John 7:39). Now, however, the baptism is complete. The way is open for the disciples to share in it — in the complete baptism which is baptism in water and the Spirit for the bearing of the sin of the world. The disciples are now taken up into that saving mission for which Jesus was anointed and sent in the power of the Spirit.

And therefore, also, they are entrusted with that authority which lies at the heart of Jesus' mission — the authority to forgive sins (20:23). The authority is given to the church (not to a ministry distinct from the church). What is being communicated here is not the revelation of a timeless truth, namely, that God forgives sin. It is the giving of a commission to do something which will otherwise remain undone: to bring the forgiveness of God to actual men and women in their concrete situations in the only way that it can be done so long as we are in the flesh — by the word and act and gesture of another human being.

The forgiveness of sins is what makes possible the gift of God's peace. The simplest and most comprehensive way of stating the content of the commission given to the church is therefore to be found in Jesus' initial word: "Peace be with you." Peace, shalom, the all-embracing blessing of Yahweh — this is what the presence of the kingdom is. The church is a movement launched into the life of the world to bear in its own life God's gift of peace for the life of the world. It is sent, therefore, not only to proclaim the kingdom, but to bear in its own life the presence of the kingdom.

II

At this point any sensitive person will be tempted to cry "Halt!" With what right can we dare to speak of the presence of the kingdom in the life of the church? When we survey the church as we know it and when we look back upon its long history of shameful betrayal, cowardly compromise, and outright wickedness, how can we dare to speak of the church as the place where God's reign is present? Are we not forced rather to remember, and to hear for ourselves, God's ancient word to his congregation: "You are a stiff-necked people; if for a single moment I should go up among you, I would consume you" (Ex. 33:5)? How can a holy and righteous God dwell in the midst of a people like this? In what sense, if at all, can we speak of the presence of the kingdom in the church? If the reign of God means the overthrow of evil and the establishment of justice, mercy, and truth, in what sense can we dare to speak of the presence of the kingdom in the church?

If we are to attempt an answer to that question, we must begin at the point which is the center of our faith — the cross. According to the witness of the New Testament, the cross is the place where to eyes of faith the reign of God is manifested in what seems to be its defect; the power of God, in weakness; the wisdom of God, in foolishness. The faith by which the church lives is that in this happening the whole frame of things has been irreversibly changed and that this is the place where the meaning of the original gospel announcement is disclosed: the kingdom of God has drawn near. The church can hold and live by this faith because this Jesus, crucified in weakness, was "designated Son of God in power according to the Spirit of holiness by his resurrection from the dead" (Rom. 1:4).

Concerning this happening three points have here to be made.

1. We are speaking about a *happening*, an event which can never be fully grasped by our intellectual powers and translated into a theory or doctrine. We are in the presence of a reality full of mystery which challenges but exceeds our grasp. A simple kind of faith has always seen the coming of the reign of God as the rejection and destruction of the enemies of Israel and the church and as the deliverance of God's people from oppression. This faith is expressed in the *vox populi* which sounds loud and clear through many passages of the Old Testament so as almost to drown the voice of the authentic prophets, who spoke often in riddles and paradoxes. It is expressed in the political messianism present among Jesus' contemporaries.

Jesus could not satisfy the *vox populi*. He outraged it. He rejected the "righteous" and accepted the "sinners." Or, to put the matter more accurately, the coming of Jesus is the shining of a light (I John 1:5) in which *all* are exposed as God's enemies, and *all* are accepted as God's beloved. Both the "righteous" — the representatives of religion, of morality, of social and political order, of sacred traditions — and the "sinners" — the "man in the street," the thoroughly "conscientized" crowd demonstrating outside the governor's mansion — are revealed in the final showdown as the murderers of God, and both are accepted as the beloved of God. "Father, forgive them; they know not what they do."

Jesus is not for one against the other. He is against all for the sake of all. Faith sees, then, in this happening the wrath of God and his love, the judgment of God and his mercy, the curse of God and his blessing. In the agony in the garden and in the cry of dereliction from the cross, where God was bereft of God for man's sake and the loving obedience which man refuses to God was offered on man's behalf, faith sees the decisive event by which all things were changed, the powers (of state, of law, of tradition) which falsely claim absolute power were unmasked and disowned, and the reign of God was established.

Down the centuries, from the first witness until today, the church has sought and used innumerable symbols to express the inexpressible mystery of the event which is the center, the crisis of all cosmic history, the hinge upon which all happenings turn. Christ the sacrifice offered for our sin, Christ the substitute standing in our place, Christ the ransom price paid for our redemption, Christ the conqueror casting out the prince of this world — these and other symbols have been used to point to the heart of the mystery. None can fully express it. It is that happening in which the reign of God is present.

2. Because it is a happening, it is part of history. It is located at a particular point of place and time in the whole vast fabric of human affairs. It happened outside Jerusalem and not outside Tokyo or Madras; in the first century and not the tenth or the twentieth. The necessary particularity of the happening is a cause of offense to millions of devout people. To millions of people — and this is especially true of those nurtured in the Indian tradition — it seems self-evident that God's presence must be equally available to all people of all times in all places. God cannot be in one place or time rather than another. God must be near to every one who turns to him. We shall have to consider the issues which this raises when we come to discuss the doctrine of election. But a preliminary word must be said here. The question at stake is as follows: Is the human counterpart of God's reign the human soul considered as a distinct monad

having an eternally unsharable destiny, or is it human history as a whole, considered as one interlocking reality within which human life has its meaning and destiny? If the former, then it follows that contingent happenings at particular times and places cannot be of ultimate significance for all human souls: the way of entry into full fruition of God's reign must be equally available to all and to each in his time and place. But if the latter is the case, if the object of God's reign is human (and cosmic) history as a whole, then the working of his reign must be such that it binds each of us to *all* as part of its very character. In that case a single happening in a particular time and place can be of decisive significance to all.

The implications of what has here been stated in a summary form must be explored in Chapter 7, but at this point we look at the one immediate consequence of our understanding of the presence of God's reign.

3. The consequence is this. The particular happening of the living, dying, and rising of Jesus, the "fact of Christ" as a happening at one time and place, must, so to say, enter into the stream of historical happenings and become part of its course. In other words, if it is true that God's reign concerns history in its unity and totality, we who live nineteen hundred years after the event must be related to it, must share in its power, not merely by reading of it in a book or hearing it in a verbal report, but by participating in the life of that society which springs from it and is continuous with it.

That this should be so is confirmed by the following facts. Jesus appears to have taken no steps to embody his teaching about the kingdom in a written form which would be insulated against distortion by the fallible memories of his disciples. The Christian church possesses nothing comparable to the Qur'an. The teaching of Jesus has come to us in varied versions filtered through the varied rememberings and interpretings of different groups of believers. What, on the other hand, did occupy the center of Jesus' concern was the calling and binding to himself of a living community of men and women who would be the witnesses of what he was and did. The new reality which he introduced into history was to be continued through history in the form of a community, not in the form of a book.

That this is so is further confirmed by the language of the earliest Christian documents. Paul's correspondence with his Christian friends is filled with phrases which express the experience of a life which is the continuing, the carrying forward of the life of the crucified and risen Jesus. We are "always carrying in the body the death of Jesus, so that the life of Jesus may be manifested in our bodies" (II Cor. 4:10). Our baptism is an identification with the dying of Jesus, so that we may walk in the new risen life which is his (Rom. 6:3–4). We died with Christ, we were raised with him, and our life is hidden in his (Col. 2:20–3:4). We are members of the "body of Christ" (I Cor. 12). All this language bears witness to the fact that there is a society in which the life of the crucified and risen Jesus lives on and his mission continues, not only as the proclamation of the kingdom but as the presence of the kingdom *in the form of death and resurrection*. It is not simply the continuance of a teaching. It would be impossible to imagine the disciples of Buddha or of Muhammed using the phrase "in Buddha" or "in Muhammed." The presence of the kingdom, hidden and revealed in the cross of Jesus, is carried through history hidden and revealed in the life of that community which bears in its life the dying and rising of Jesus.

4. Hidden and revealed? Certainly no one will question the first of these two words. One need not be a cynic to ask whether the church's long history of betrayal has not hidden the presence of the kingdom so effectively as to destroy it. It is important to remember how relentlessly the New Testament emphasizes the reality of sin in the church. In every strand of the New Testament we are confronted with the fact that sin, betrayal, or compromise is no accidental or subsequent or unoriginal accretion but has been at the heart of the church from the beginning. In the Synoptic traditions Peter, who is the first to confess Christ, is also the first to reject the way Christ must go — the way of the cross. The

great promise which played so central a role in the teaching of the church, "You are Peter, and on this rock I will build my church," is followed instantly by a terrible rebuke, "Get behind me, Satan" (Matt. 16:18, 23). Would that Michelangelo's great dome at St. Peter's had been designed to make room for both of those texts, for one without the other can only deceive! Paul's letters, likewise, are relentless in exposing the sin of those very communities which in the same letter he hails as the temple of God (I Cor. 3:16–17) and the body of Christ (I Cor. 6:15). Above all, the fourth Gospel insists with almost unbearable reiteration that in the person of Judas the devil has been at work from the foundation of the church. But not only in the person of Judas is this true. A comparison of John 6:66–70 with Matthew 16:21–23 suggests that the identification is not so simple. The same dark shadow plays across the scene in the upper room when Jesus solemnly foretold his betrayal by one of his chosen friends, and "the disciples looked at one another, uncertain of whom he spoke" (John 13:22; cf. Mark 14:19 where the disciples "[began] to say to him one after another: 'Is it I?' "). If the church is the bearer of the presence of the kingdom through history, it is surely not as the community of the righteous in a sinful world. To imagine that would be to fall victim again to the seduction of the *vox populi* against which the prophets testified and of which the cross of Jesus is the final contradiction. The presence of the kingdom is a hidden presence, hidden in the cross of Jesus, but precisely in its hiddenness it is revealed to those to whom God through his Spirit grants the gift of faith. If we say — as we must — that the reign of God was present in Jesus, that it was present in his living, his dying, and his risen life, we have to go on to say that in a secondary, derivative, but nonetheless real sense the reign of God is present (hidden yet revealed to eyes of faith) in the community which bears his name, lives by faith in his person and work, is anointed by his Spirit, and lives through history the dying and rising of Jesus. It is a sinful community. It is, during most of its history, a weak, divided, and unsuccessful community. But because it is the community which lives by and bears witness to the risen life of the crucified Lord, it is the place where the reign of God is actually present and at work in the midst of history, and where the mission of Jesus is being accomplished. This affirmation is not made as the conclusion of a survey of the history of the church and its present reality. On the contrary, it is made as an integral part of the confession of faith. Because I believe in one God the Father, one Lord Jesus Christ, and one Holy Spirit, I believe in one holy catholic and apostolic church. And I believe that the reign of God is present in the midst of this sinful, weak, and divided community, not through any power or goodness of its own, but because God has called and chosen this company of people to be the bearers of his gift on behalf of all men.

At the heart of the life of the church is the eucharistic celebration, in which those who gather around the Lord's table are taken up again and again into his sacrificial action, made partakers of his dying and of his risen life, consecrated afresh to the Father in and through him, and sent out into the world to bear the power of cross and resurrection through the life of the world. This is how the Eucharist is interpreted in the great consecration prayer (John 17). The church represents the presence of the reign of God in the life of the world, not in the triumphalist sense (as the "successful" cause) and not in the moralistic sense (as the "righteous"cause), but in the sense that it is the place where the mystery of the kingdom present in the dying and rising of Jesus is made present here and now so that all people, righteous and unrighteous, are enabled to taste and share the love of God before whom all are unrighteous and all are accepted as righteous. It is the place where the glory of God ("glory as of an only son") actually abides among men so that the love of God is actually available to sin-burdened men and women (John 17:22–23). It is the place where the power of God is manifested in a community of sinners. It is the place where the promise of Jesus is fulfilled: "I, when I am lifted up from the earth, will draw all men to myself"

60

(John 12:32). It is the place where the reign of God is present as love shared among the unlovely.

There are places, as there always have been, where the church is precluded from any kind of public proclamation of the gospel or any kind of public service. In such places as, for example, the Soviet Union today, the mission of Christ is continued through the silent but powerful attraction of communities which live by the weekly celebration of the eucharistic mystery and which draw into their fellowship men and women moved by the real presence of the love of God in the midst of the life of the world. There is little opportunity to proclaim the reign of God; its presence is its own witness.

6

Bearing the Witness of the Spirit: Mission as Hope in Action

I HAVE SPOKEN of mission as the *proclaiming* of God's kingship over all human history and over the whole cosmos. Mission is concerned with nothing less than the completion of all that God has begun to do in the creation of the world and of man. Its concern is not sectional but total and universal.

I have spoken, secondly, of mission as the *presence* of God and kingship in Jesus and in the church. In this aspect mission is concerned with the limited, the particular, the contingent.

Now it is essential to add a third affirmation, without which the first two would be misleading. I have affirmed that God's kingship is present in the church; but it must be insisted that it is not the property of the church. It is not domesticated within the church. Mission is not simply the self-propagation of the church by the putting forth of the power which inheres in its life. To accept that picture would be to sanction an appalling distortion of mission. On the contrary, the active agent of mission is a power which rules, guides, and goes before the church: the free, sovereign, living power of the Spirit of God. Mission is not just something which the church does; it is something which is done by the Spirit who is himself the witness, who

62

changes both the world and the church, who always goes
before the church in her missionary journey. It is therefore
not enough to speak of the proclamation of the kingdom and
of the presence of the kingdom; we must also speak of the
prevenience, the previousness of the kingdom. To explore this
third dimension of mission will be the business of this
chapter.

A very quick glance at the New Testament evidence will
serve as a reminder of the central place which the work of
the Spirit must have in any systematic thought about
mission.

"Spirit" is the word used in English versions of the Bible
to translate the Hebrew word *ruach*, meaning "wind" or
"breath." A man's breath is the secret of his life, and the
Spirit of the Lord (*ruach Yahweh*) is the very life of the Lord
himself put forth to give life and power, wisdom and
speech, knowledge and understanding to man. It is the living, mighty, self-communicating presence of God himself.

From the very beginning of the New Testament, the
coming of Jesus, his words and works are connected directly with the power of the Spirit. It is by the Spirit that
Jesus is conceived, by the Spirit that he is anointed at his
baptism, by the Spirit that he is driven into the desert for
his encounter with Satan. It is in the power of the Spirit
that he enters upon his ministry of teaching and healing
(Luke 4:14, 18; Matt. 12:18). In view of all this it is
noteworthy that the Gospels are totally silent about any
communication of the Spirit to the disciples during the
period of Jesus' earthly ministry. It is only when the baptism initiated in the Jordan has been filled out in the ministry of Jesus and consummated in his death that the disciples
can enter into the new anointing of the Spirit through their
identification with the risen Jesus. I have already referred
to the Johannine account of this (John 20:19–23), and we
shall now look at the Lucan account in the Acts of the
Apostles (which might well be entitled "The Acts of the
Spirit"), in which, above all, we have the full exposition of
the work of the Spirit as the real agent of mission.

At the very beginning of the book the disciples are told to await the completion of what had been begun by John's baptism in the Jordan. "John baptized with water, but before many days you shall be baptized with the Holy Spirit" (Acts 1:5). John's baptism had been a sign pointing to the coming presence of the reality of the kingdom. In the baptism of Jesus sign and reality met. His baptism was baptism in water and the Spirit. The two are now one (John 3:5), and what God has joined shall not again be put asunder. Their baptism could not be complete until his was fully accomplished (cf. Luke 12:50). Now their time has come and they will share his complete baptism, which is the one baptism for the sin of the world.

Does that mean, then, that the time of waiting is over? If the sign and the reality have become one, does that not mean that the Day of the Lord is here? "Will you at this time restore the kingdom to Israel?" (1:6) is a reasonable question. The answer is a warning and a promise. The warning is that God has his own infinite patience and it is not for men to try to foreclose on his promises (1:7). The promise is that the disciples will immediately be given, not the kingdom in its fullness, but that gift which is the foretaste, the pledge, the guarantee of the kingdom — namely, the presence of the Spirit (Acts 1:8; cf. II Cor. 1:22; Eph. 1:14). The word used in these two latter passages, *arrabōn*, is a commercial word denoting a cash deposit paid as the pledge of the full amount to be paid later. The disciples are not promised the full victory of God's kingdom now; they *are* promised immediately the *arrabōn* — the advance installment which will make them the living evidences of the reality which is promised. The real presence of God's own life lived in their common life will be the evidence, the witness to all the nations, that the full reality of God's victorious reign is on the way. What is given here (and this is vital for true missionary thinking) is not a command, but a promise. The presence of the Spirit will make them witnesses.

This promise is fulfilled on the day of Pentecost. The disciples are now given the same anointing which Jesus received at his baptism. And the disciples know that this is indeed the "Day of the Lord" to which the prophets had looked forward. "The last days" have dawned (Acts 2:17). The curse of Babel is being removed. The blessing of God promised to all nations in the primal covenant with Noah is now available to all (2:21). Men of every nation are able to hear in their own tongues the mighty works of God (2:11). The gathering of all the nations to be the people of the Lord and of his Messiah has begun.

It is thus by an action of the sovereign Spirit of God that the church is launched on its mission. And it remains the mission of the Spirit. He is central. It is he who brings about the meeting of Philip with the finance minister of Ethiopia (8:26–40). It is the Spirit who prepares Ananias to receive the archpersecutor Saul as a brother (9:10–19) and who prepares Peter to break his cherished principles and go to be the guest of a pagan army officer (10:1–20). It is the Spirit who initiates the first mission to the Gentiles (13:1–2) and guides the missionaries in their journeys (16:7).

The story of the meeting of Peter and Cornelius is especially significant in the light which it throws on the sovereign work of the Spirit in mission. It has been rightly said that this is the story not only of the conversion of Cornelius but also of the conversion of Peter and of the church. At the beginning of the story we see Peter firmly rejecting what seems to be an assault on his fidelity to the law (10:9–16). His whole identity as a son of Israel is bound up with strict obedience to the commandments. But despite these scruples he is persuaded to go to the home of the heathen officer and to tell him the gospel story. Before he has finished the situation passes out of his control. Cornelius and his household are caught up, in a way which cannot be gainsaid, into the same experience of freedom and joy which Peter and the others have known since Pentecost. Peter understands that he is not in control. A power greater than his own has broken down the hedge which protected devout Jews from the uncleanness of the heathen world. Peter can do nothing but humbly accept the fact and receive these uncircumcised pagans by baptism into the fellowship of the church (10:47–48).

In the following chapter we find Peter having to defend his action before the church. What he has done is a clear breach of the law under which Israel lives. His defense is simply to recount the undeniable activities of the Spirit by which he has been led, and to conclude: "Who was I that I could withstand God?" (11:17).

What the story makes clear, and what is spelled out in more theological terms (as we shall see) in the fourth Gospel, is that mission changes not only the world but also the church. Quite plainly in this case there is a conversion of the church as well as the conversion of Cornelius. It is not as though the church opened its gates to admit a new person into its company, and then closed them again, remaining unchanged except for the addition of a name to its roll of members. Mission is not just church extension. It is something more costly and more revolutionary. It is the action of the Holy Spirit who in his sovereign freedom both convicts the world (John 16:8–11) and leads the church toward the fullness of the truth which it has not yet grasped (John 16:12–15). Mission is not essentially an action by which the church puts forth its own power and wisdom to conquer the world around it; it is, rather, an action of God, putting forth the power of his Spirit to bring the universal work of Christ for the salvation of the world nearer to its completion. At the end of the story, which runs from Acts 10:1 to 11:18, the church itself became a kind of society different from what it was before Peter and Cornelius met. It had been a society enclosed within the cultural world of Israel: it became something radically different — a society which spanned the enormous gulf between Jew and pagan and was open to embrace all the nations which had been outside the covenant by which Israel lived.

The story of Peter and Cornelius is the preface to the much wider and more costly struggle which had to be fought out concerning the conditions on which Gentile converts should be admitted to the church. Those who insisted upon circumcision had an enormously strong case. The law of circumcision was the most fundamental element in the whole structure of the law. The uncircumcised male was excommunicated from God's people (Gen. 17:14). Martyrs had given their lives to uphold this law. Jesus himself had been circumcised, and by no single word had he suggested that circumcision was to be set aside. There was nothing in the tradition to be compared with Jesus' attitude to that other foundation pillar of the law — the Sabbath. Those who insisted that circumcision was an indispensable condition for membership in the household of God had overwhelmingly strong reasons to support their case. To talk of uncircumcised pagans being heirs of Abraham and members of the household of God was, it could well be argued, to make nonsense of the plain teaching of Scripture, of tradition, and even of Jesus himself.

What arguments could lead the church to set aside such an overwhelming weight of authority? Only the argument of fact — the fact, namely, that through the preaching of Christ, God's own Spirit had been manifestly and unmistakably given to uncircumcised pagans. At the crucial point in his argument with the Galatians Paul writes: "Let me ask you only this: Did you receive the Spirit by works of the law or by hearing with faith?" (Gal. 3:2). There is only one possible reply, and it settles the matter. So also in the debate about the matter reported in Acts 15, the crucial word which settles the matter is Peter's own recalling of his earlier experience: "God who knows the heart bore witness to them, giving them the Holy Spirit just as he did to us" (Acts 15:8). After this we read that "All the assembly kept silence" as they listened to the story of God's mighty works among the uncircumcised heathen through the preaching of the gospel (15:12).

At this point the church has to keep silence. It is not in control of the mission. There is another who is in control, and his fresh works will repeatedly surprise the church, compelling it to stop talking and to listen. Because the Spirit himself is sovereign over the mission, the church can only

67

be the attentive servant. In sober truth the Spirit is himself the witness who goes before the church in its missionary journey. The church's witness is secondary and derivative. The church is witness insofar as it follows obediently where the Spirit leads.

This picture of the relation of the Spirit to the church's mission is expounded theologically in other parts of the New Testament. Let me briefly refer to some of the abundant material bearing on this.

The "Little Apocalypse" of Mark contains a saying which is paralleled in Matthew and Luke: Christians will be put on trial for their testimony but are not to be anxious about their defense; the right words will be given them, "for it is not you who speak, but the Holy Spirit" (Mark 13:11; cf. Matt. 10:20 and Luke 21:14–15). This idea that the Holy Spirit is the advocate who stands in court to speak on behalf of the Christian under trial is further developed in the discourses which are the Johannine equivalent of the Marcan apocalypse. The Spirit is the advocate who will stand by the disciples when the protecting presence of Jesus is removed (John 14:16–20). He will be there to bring to their remembrance the words and works of Jesus (14:26). The world will hate them and reject their teaching, but in this context of rejection there will be an advocate to stand by them in their trial, and his witness cannot be silenced; because of this powerful witness, their witness will stand (15:18–27). In fact this advocate will do more than defend them: he will confute their adversaries, proving to the accusing world that its fundamental religious and moral convictions are wrong and are proved wrong by the work of Jesus (16:8–11). And finally this advocate will lead the disciples into the fullness of the truth because he will bring "all that the Father has" and declare it to the church as the rightful patrimony of Jesus (16:12–15). In Paul's words, he will bring every thought into captivity to Christ (II Cor. 10:5).

This picture of the mission of the church is as remote as possible from the picture of the church as a powerful body putting forth its strength and wisdom to master the strength and wisdom of the world. The case is exactly the opposite. The church is weak. It is under trial. It does not know what to say. It has no arguments to confute its persecutors. But exactly in this situation it can be calmly confident. It does not have to conduct its own defense. There is an advocate who is more than adequate for the task. It is his work — and he is quite capable of it — to take the weakness and foolishness of the cross, mirrored in the life of the community, and make it the witness that turns the world upside down and confutes its most fundamental notions. Because he knows this Paul can exult in the assurance that "when I am weak, then I am strong" (II Cor. 12:1–10). Because he knows this the writer of the Apocalypse sees as the triumphant army of the Lord those who have suffered to the limit of human endurance and sees on the throne of the universe the slain Lamb. Because we know this we can be assured that the mission of the church is not conducted, nor is its success measured, after the manner of a military operation or a sales campaign. The witness which confutes the world is not ours; it is that of one greater than ourselves who goes before us. Our task is simply to follow faithfully.

The real triumphs of the gospel have not been won when the church is strong in a worldly sense; they have been won when the church is faithful in the midst of weakness, contempt, and rejection. And I would simply add my own testimony, which could be illustrated by many examples, that it has been in situations where faithfulness to the gospel placed the church in a position of total weakness and rejection that the advocate has himself risen up and, often through the words and deeds of very "insignificant" people, spoken the word that confronted and shamed the wisdom and power of the world.

Paul's writings give us further illumination of the role of the Spirit in the mission of the church. In referring to the promise of the Spirit in Acts 1:6–8, which is given in response to a question about the immediate coming of the kingdom, I drew attention to the word *arrabōn* which Paul uses to describe the Spirit. The gift of the Spirit is related to the coming of the kingdom as cash-in-advance is related to the full settlement of an account. The Spirit is a foretaste of the messianic feast. The presence of the Spirit is a real presence of love, joy, and peace which belong to God's perfect reign, but it is not yet the fullness of these things. It is the sign that the last things have begun (Acts 2:17); consequently it both assures us of their coming and makes us hope more eagerly for their full fruition. It is in this way that the presence of the Spirit brings a powerful witness to the reality of the reign of God to which the world is otherwise blind.

The same idea is developed through another set of symbols in Paul's treatment of the Spirit in Romans 8. By the action of God in Jesus Christ we have been set free from the rule of sin and death and placed under the rule of the Spirit, for all "liberation" is a change of government (8:2). This new life under the regime of the Spirit holds out the promise not only of the renewal of our whole personalities (8:10) but of the liberation of the whole creation from the domination of false powers (8:19–21). The gift of the Spirit is the "first fruit" which assures us that the full harvest is to come (8:22–24). Having been made children of God through the Spirit of him who enables us to say *Abba,* we know that we are heirs and therefore look forward to the full possession of our inheritance (8:14–17). Our true standing as sons and heirs will be authenticated by our participation in the sufferings of Jesus. Once again, as in the Johannine discourses, it is in the midst of the world's rejection and of the messianic tribulations which flow from it that we are assured of the presence of the Spirit. The Spirit brings the reality of the new world to come into the midst of the old world that is. It is the firstfruit of the coming harvest. It is the proof that we are heirs of the coming kingdom. And it is thus that the Spirit is witness — the recognizable presence of a future which is promised but is not yet in sight. It is thus, also, that the Spirit is the source of hope — not just hope for ourselves, but hope for the completion of God's whole cosmic work. "In this hope we are saved" (8:24). It is because of this hope that we are liable to be invited "to account for the hope that is in [us]" (I Pet. 3:15) and so to become involved in the missionary dialogue. Seen from this point of view, mission might be defined as "hope in action." It is the whole way of living, acting, and speaking which arises from the fact that we have already received the first installment of the promised treasure, the firstfruit of the promised harvest, and can therefore work and wait with both eagerness and patience for the fullness of what God has promised for his whole creation. The witness of which the New Testament passages speak is God's gift, not our accomplishment. It is not a light that we kindle and carry, shielding its flame from the winds; it is the light that shines on us because our faces are turned towards the radiance which is already lighting up the eastern sky with the promise of a new day.

The reign of God which the church proclaims is indeed also present in the life of the church, but it is not the church's possession. It goes before us, summoning us to follow. The practical implications of this will be discussed in a later chapter. Here it is enough to say that the picture given us in the Acts is one that is constantly being reproduced in the missionary experience of the church. It is the Holy Spirit who leads the way, opening a door here which the church must then obediently enter, kindling a flame there which the church must lovingly tend.

My own experience as a missionary has been that the significant advances of the church have not been the result of our own decisions about the mobilizing and allocating of "resources." This kind of language, appropriate for a military campaign or a commercial enterprise, is not appropriate here. The significant advances in my experience have come through happenings of which the story of Peter and Cornelius is a paradigm. In ways of which we have no advance knowledge, God opens the heart of a man or woman to the gospel. The messenger (the "angel" of Acts 10:3) may be a stranger, a preacher, a piece of Scripture, a dream, an answered prayer, or a deep experience of joy or sorrow, of danger or deliverance. It was no part of any missionary "strategy" devised by the church. It was the free and sovereign deed of God who goes before his church. And, like Peter, the church can usually find good reasons for being unwilling to follow. But follow it must if it is to be faithful. For the mission is not ours but God's.

*   *   *   *   *

From "the beginning of the gospel" (Mark 1:1) when Jesus came into Galilee preaching the kingdom of God, the concern of mission is nothing less than this: the kingdom of God, the sovereign rule of the Father of Jesus over all humankind and over all creation. I have spoken of mission in three ways. It is the proclamation of the kingdom, the presence of the kingdom, and the prevenience of the kingdom. By proclaiming the reign of God over all things the church acts out its faith that the Father of Jesus is indeed ruler of all. The church, by inviting all humankind to share in the mystery of the presence of the kingdom hidden in its life through its union with the crucified and risen life of Jesus, acts out the love of Jesus which took him to the cross. By obediently following where the Spirit leads, often in ways neither planned, known, nor understood, the church acts out the hope which it is given by the presence of the Spirit who is the living foretaste of the kingdom.

This threefold way of understanding the church's mission is rooted in the triune being of God himself. If any one of these is taken in isolation as the clue to the understanding of mission, distortion follows.

In succeeding chapters I shall use this threefold model as a framework for the discussion of some of the theoretical and practical problems that the church must meet in pursuing its missionary calling.

7

The Gospel and World History

THE GOSPEL which Jesus preached is the good news of
God's universal reign. It is directed to the whole human
and cosmic reality. And yet it is also bound up with particular names of people and places belonging to particular cultures. It speaks of the story of Israel, one people among all
the peoples, and of the man whose Hebrew name was
Joshua, one man among all the billions who have lived. Its
language and its fundamental symbols belong to the cultural
world of the eastern Mediterranean, and therefore in the
cultural worlds of Africa, India, or Japan they are foreign.

I have referred in passing to this scandal of particularity,
and now we must face it squarely. To a devout Hindu, heir
to 4000 years of profound religious and philosophical experience, there is something truly scandalous in the suggestion that, to put it crudely, he must import the necessities
for his soul's salvation from abroad. "Is it really credible,"
he will ask, "that the Supreme Being whom I and my
forefathers have loved and worshiped for forty centuries, is
incapable of meeting my soul's need, and that I must await
the coming of an agent of another tradition from Europe or
North America if I am to receive his salvation? What kind of
a god are you asking me to believe in? Is he not simply the
projection of your own culture-bound prejudices? Come!
Let us be reasonable! Let us open our treasures and put

them side by side, and we shall see that your symbols and mine are but the differing forms of one reality shaped according to our different histories and cultures. If God is truly God — God of all peoples and all the earth — then surely God can and will save me where I am with the means he has provided for me in the long experience of my own people."

Who can deny the reasonableness of this plea? And one does not need to go to India to hear it. It can be put with equal force to the missionary who proposes to go, not to India, but into the factory or dockyard of his own city. "Don't imagine," he will be told, "that you are going to take God into the factory. He is there already. He has been at work there long before you came on the scene and he will be there after you have gone. Your job is to learn what he is doing in the world which is already his, not to introduce him to a world from which he is absent."

The scandal of particularity is at the center of the question of missions. To be more precise, it is the problem of relating God's universality to his particular deeds and words. God is over all and in all, and not a sparrow falls to the ground without his will. Yet the Bible talks of God acting and God speaking in particular times and places. How are these related? With what propriety can we speak of particular acts of God if God is universal Lord of all? How can we relate this universality to this particularity?

The attentive reader of the Bible will note how constantly these two themes are interwoven without any apparent sense of incompatibility. In Romans 10:12–13 Paul makes a statement of sweeping universality: "There is no distinction between Jew and Greek; the same Lord is Lord of all and bestows his riches upon all who call upon him. For, 'everyone who calls on the name of the Lord will be saved.' " But this leads him straight into the assertion of the need for the missionary to go and preach (Rom. 10:14–15). In John 4:24, the text which has often been used to deny the need for "form or sign or ritual word" in religion, "God is Spirit, and they that worship him must worship him in

spirit and in truth," follows immediately on the blunt
statement which describes the Samaritan worship as igno-
rant and asserts that "salvation is from the Jews" (4:22).
Universality and particularity do not contradict one another
but require one another. How can this be so?

I

The answer is to be found in the doctrine which per-
meates and controls the whole Bible — the doctrine of
election. From the beginning of the Bible to its end we are
presented with the story of a universal purpose carried out
through a continuous series of particular choices. God, according to the biblical picture, although he is the creator,
ruler, sustainer, and judge of all peoples, does not accomplish his purpose of blessing for all peoples by means of
a revelation simultaneously and equally available to all. He
chooses one to be the bearer of his blessing for the many.
Abraham is chosen to be the pioneer of faith and so to
receive the blessing through which all nations will be
blessed. Moses is chosen to be the agent of Israel's redemption; Israel is chosen to be a kingdom of priests for the whole
earth. The disciples are chosen that they may be "fishers of
men" (Mark 1:17) or, in another metaphor, that they may
"go and bear fruit" (John 15:16). The church is a body
chosen "to declare the wonderful deeds" of God (I Pet. 2:9).
    This is the pattern throughout the Bible. The key to the
relation between the universal and the particular is God's
way of election. The one (or the few) is chosen for the sake
of the many; the particular is chosen for the sake of the
universal.
    To speak about the doctrine of election is to risk a curt
dismissal. There are enough reasons in the history of Christian thought to explain the disfavor in which the doctrine is
held. And today we must add the fact that any suggestion of
limited privilege touches the raw nerves of contemporary
bourgeois guilt. "Elitism" is the unforgivable sin. Why,
then, should we burden a discussion of mission with the

doctrine of election? What is at stake?

1. What is at stake is the full integrity of our nature as human beings. If that seems a surprising statement, look again at the initial protest. What lies behind the deep, emotionally charged protest of the man who asks: "Why must I look elsewhere for the source of my soul's salvation? Why cannot God deal with me as I am, as the person I am with the cultural and religious identity that I have?" At the heart of that protest there is the conviction that my own identity and my own destiny are, in the last analysis, mine alone. It is no accident that this protest has been most clearly articulated in India, for in no part of the world has the eternal significance of the human soul been so resolutely affirmed as in India, and the Indian experience has deeply influenced Western thought through many contacts over two and a half millennia. The two most influential philosophical schools in Hinduism have been the Samkhya and the Vedanta. According to the former, all reality exists in two forms — the physical and the spiritual. The latter consists of an infinite number of personal monads which have been enmeshed (for example, through a human body) in the physical world. Liberation, in this perspective, means the disentanglement of the soul from its involvement in the world of nature so that it may achieve its proper freedom as an independent monad. According to the Vedanta as developed in its most logical form by Shankara, the ultimate reality is identical with the true self, not the self which can be the object of thought, but the self which is the eternal subject, pure consciousness, pure spirit. Although there are thus very important differences between these two systems, they are at one in understanding the central being of the human person as a spiritual monad which does not require either other persons or a created world for the achievement of its true destiny. Salvation, or liberation, or realization concerns the soul as a pure monad. Man is ultimately spiritual, and the world of things and of other persons is marginal to his eternal destiny.

The biblical vision of man's nature and destiny is very

different. The human in the Bible exists only in relationship with other persons and only as part of the created
world. In both the creation stories of Genesis these two
points are insisted upon. Humanity exists only in the double
form of man and woman. The image of God is present in this
relatedness-in-love (Gen. 1:27). And it is immediately
added that "God blessed them and said to them: 'Be fruitful
and multiply and fill the earth and subdue it'" (1:28).
Human life from its beginning is a life of shared relationship
in the context of a task — a task which is continuous with
God's creative work in the natural world. In contrast to
those forms of spirituality which seek the "real" self by
looking within, the Bible invites us to see the real human
life as a life of shared relationships in a world of living
creatures and created things, a life of mutual personal responsibility in the context of a shared responsibility for the
created world, its animal and vegetable life and its resources of soil and water and air. This, and no other, is the
real human life, which is the object of God's primal blessing
and of his saving purpose. Consequently, the vision with
which the Bible closes is not the vision of a purely
"spiritual" existence, but the vision of a city. The city is the
symbol of man's supreme achievements in "subduing the
earth," as it is also the scene of his most horrible perversions
of that divine commission. The city of the Apocalypse is a
gift of God, not a product of man's wisdom. But it is a city,
and the city is the place where man's calling to mutual
relatedness and man's commission to subdue the earth have
their sharpest focus.

In short, the Bible invites us to see the really human, but
not by looking within and finding at the core of human
reality a purely spiritual entity which is the object of God's
saving purpose. On the contrary, it invites us to see the
really human as the life of mutual responsibility in the
context of a shared responsibility for the created world and
therefore to see God's saving purpose in terms of this real
world of real people.

And this is so because God is no solitary monad. The

unreal picture of man as an isolated spiritual monad belongs to the same world of thought as the picture of God as an isolated spiritual monad. The reality is not so; God, as he is revealed to us in the gospel, is not a monad. Interpersonal relatedness belongs to the very being of God. Therefore there can be no salvation for man except in relatedness. No one can be made whole except by being restored to the wholeness of that being-in-relatedness for which God made man and the world and which is the image of that being-in-relatedness which is the being of God himself. A glimpse of this is given to us in the consecration prayer (John 17) where Jesus prays that those who believe may be made part of the very unity of the divine being, united by that which binds the Father and the Son, which is nothing other than the glory of God (20–23).

The biblical insistence that God's universal purpose of salvation is accomplished through the choosing of particular people arises from this fundamental insight concerning the nature of man. If each human being is to be ultimately understood as an independent spiritual monad, then salvation could only be through an action directed impartially to each and all. But if the truly human is the shared reality of mutual and collective responsibility which the Bible envisages, then salvation must be an action which binds us together and restores for us the true mutual relation to each other and the true shared relation to the world of nature. This would mean that the gift of salvation would be bound up with our openness to one another. It would have to pass from one to the other. It would not come to each, direct from above, like a shaft of light through the roof. It would come from the neighbor in the action by which we open the door to invite the neighbor in. But the neighbor would have to be sent (Rom. 10:14). There would have to be one called and chosen to be the bearer of the blessing. The blessing is intended for all. But the blessing itself would be negated if it were not given and received in a way that binds each to the other. God's way of universal salvation, if it is to be addressed to man as he really is and not to the unreal abstraction of a detached "soul," must be accomplished by the way of election — of choosing, calling, and sending one to be the bearer of blessing for all. The biblical doctrine of election is fundamental to any doctrine of mission which is addressed to men and women as they really are in the fullness of their shared life in history and in nature.

In one of the glowing passages of the New Testament where the universality of God's purpose and the particularity of his calling are brought together in a single vision (Eph. 1:3–14) the writer speaks of the cosmic range of God's purpose but links it firmly to God's action in choosing and calling a particular people. The purpose which God has in view is nothing less than the uniting of the whole cosmos ("all things in earth and heaven") with Christ as their head (1:10). It is for this cosmic purpose that "he chose us in Christ before the foundation of the world" (1:4). The choosing is "in Christ" and not otherwise. There is no election apart from Christ, as some theologies have seemed to suggest. Christ is himself the chosen one, the beloved who was acclaimed as such at his baptism, but was in truth the beloved Son of the Father from before the foundation of the world. It is through him and in him that those little companies of believers in Ephesus and the other Asian cities have been chosen, "destined in love" (1:5), "appointed to live for the praise of his glory" (1:12), and entrusted with the understanding of the "mystery" of God's purpose to "unite all things in Christ" (1:9–10). It is all the action of the Father, who has freely chosen them in his beloved Son and assured them of the completion of what he has begun by giving them the Spirit — "the guarantee of our inheritance until we acquire possession of it" (1:14). The whole action has its origin in the eternal being of the triune God before the creation; it has its goal in the final unity of the whole creation in Christ; and meanwhile the secret of this cosmic plan, the foretaste of its completion, have been entrusted to these little communities of marginal people scattered through the towns and cities of Asia Minor.

To any cultivated pagan who chanced to read this letter,

79

the contrast between the vision of a vast cosmic purpose and the present reality of pitifully weak and insignificant community drawn (apparently) from the least influential elements in society, must have seemed laughable. To many in later ages, especially when these little communities had grown into powerful institutions, it has seemed not merely laughable but scandalous and immoral. Can it really be believed that God, who is creator of heaven and earth, by whom and for whom all things exist, has concentrated his purpose of salvation on these miniscule communities in the little world of the eastern Mediterranean, leaving the millions in China and India and Africa, who at the same moment are living, praying, suffering, and dying, outside of the realm of salvation until they are "discovered," many centuries too late, by the explorers and missionaries of these chosen people? If this doctrine of the election of a chosen people appointed to be the bearers of salvation for all mankind seems intolerable to many sincere Christians in the twentieth century, has it not really been intolerable from the beginning?

2. If we are to respond to this protest we must take account of the distortion and misunderstandings of the biblical teaching about election which have through the centuries given just ground for the protest. If these can be clearly identified, the way will be open for a restatement of the doctrine of election which will show the true relation between the universal and the particular in God's work of salvation.

(a) God, according to the Bible, purposes the salvation of all. "He desires all men to be saved and to come to the knowledge of the truth" (I Tim. 2:4). His primal covenant of blessing is for all, without conditions, and it includes the blessing of the earth for man's sake (Gen. 9:1–17). But when men forfeit this blessing by their self-confident imperialism (Gen. 11:1–9), God chooses one of the families of mankind to be the bearer of the blessing on behalf of all (Gen. 12:1–3). This family is in no way superior to the rest of the human race. The ancient stories repeatedly emphasize that the conduct of the "pagan" is more noble and righteous than that of the elect. One could cite, for example, the contrasting conduct of Abraham and Pharaoh (Gen. 12:10–20), of Isaac and Abimelech (26:1–11), of Jacob and Esau (compare Gen. 27 with 33), and the story of Jonah already discussed. But the Old Testament repeatedly portrays the chosen people as falling into the illusion that they have a privileged position with God which insures them against disaster. Through the repeated hammer blows of defeat, destruction, and deportation, interpreted by the faithful prophets, Israel has to learn that election is not for comfort and security but for suffering and humiliation. As blow follows blow there is the repeated temptation to think that Yahweh has forgotten his covenant and abandoned his people. But again and again there is a prophetic call to recognize the hand of God who will never cancel his covenant but whose unshakable purpose it is that Israel shall be the witness that manifests his sovereign glory to all the nations. Israel's election means that she is called to be servant and witness of Yahweh for all the nations, not to be ruler and mistress of the nations. To be the elect is a fearful responsibility.

(b) There is a further and more subtle way in which election can be and was misunderstood. It is at the center of the struggle which Paul waged with those who insisted upon circumcision as a necessary condition for membership in the church. It is also at the heart of many of the perplexities which surround the discussion of the uniqueness and universality of the gospel today.

At the center of the story of the Bible is the fact of God's covenant with Israel. God not only chose and called Israel among all the nations; he also bound Israel to himself in a covenant of which the visible sign was circumcision. When the covenant was renewed after the deliverance from Egypt there was annexed to it ("added" is Paul's word in Gal. 3:19) the body of instruction which is usually referred to as "the law." But what is the relation between the law and the covenant? Is the law attached to the covenant in such a way that the former conditions the latter, that is to

81

say, that the blessing promised in the covenant is conditional upon fulfillment of the law? This seems to be the natural and indeed the obvious way to understand it. A covenant implies two parties. Both sides must keep it. Those whom God chooses to call into a covenant relation with himself are certainly called to a fearful responsibility. There is no question here of a privilege which does not carry the corresponding responsibility. But surely we can argue that if the elect do keep the law and so fulfill their part in the covenant, then they do have a privilege which the pagan, outside of the covenant, does not have.

This seems obvious. It seemed obvious to the Jewish Christians with whom Paul was in controversy. If it is true that God has chosen Israel to be his covenant people, and if he has attached to the covenant laws which are binding on the covenant partners, and if I am an Israelite who keeps these laws, then surely I have a standing before God which the pagan, who is outside the covenant and does not keep the law, cannot claim.

Paul armed himself with all the reason and passion of which he was capable in order to demolish this position. *No one* can claim rights against God. No one can claim privilege with God which is denied to others. There is no partiality with God. He will judge all alike, Jew and pagan, all by the same measure (Rom. 2). "There is no distinction between Jew and Greek; the same Lord is Lord of all and bestows his riches upon all who call upon him" (Rom. 10:12). The covenant is not a contract. It is an action of pure free grace. In its initial form as given to Abraham it is simply a free promise of universal blessing which is to embrace all the nations (Gal. 3:8). It is not a contract which offers a conditional promise provided that the law is kept. The law is *not* part of the covenant (Gal. 3:15-18). What is it then? What is its place in God's dealing with Israel? Paul's answer to this deserves careful attention.

He characterizes the role of the law in a threefold way (Gal. 3:19-29): "It was added because of transgressions, till the offspring should come to whom the promise had been made; and it was ordained by angels through an intermediary."

(i) It was added "because of transgressions." This strange phrase becomes clear if we look at the whole argument and at the related argument of Romans 5:18-21. In fact all — Israel and the pagan world — fall short of God's glory. Nowhere is there a kind of human living which simply reflects the glory of the Trinity. Law performs the function of bringing this fact to clear expression. It destroys any possibility of a claim against God. It destroys the possibility of construing the covenant as a contract. It closes every door for men and women except the one which God has opened — the way of free, sovereign, overflowing kindness. It "shuts up all under sin in order to have mercy on all" (Rom. 11:32).

(ii) The law was added "till the offspring should come." It is provisional, that is, it looks forward to that by which it will be superseded, namely, that relationship of sonship which is made possible by the coming of the Son. He alone can bring us directly into the life which the law cannot offer — a participation in the glory of the Trinity (Gal. 4:6; cf. John 1:14 and 17:22-23).

(iii) The law was "ordained by angels." To Jewish piety the tradition that angels participated in the revelation of the law on Sinai was a symbol of its transcendent greatness. For Paul it is an evidence of the fact that in the law we are not dealing directly with the being of God but with one of the subordinate agencies (the "powers" to which God allows a limited and delegated authority over human affairs; cf. I Cor. 2:5-8; Rom. 13:1-6; Col. 2:15). For those who have been liberated by Christ to allow the law again to control them means to accept the slavery of "beings that by nature are no gods" (Gal. 4:8).

To summarize Paul's argument, then, the covenant is not to be turned into a contract. It is not a bargain which will entitle a man to claim rights from God on the ground that he has fulfilled its conditions. The covenant is an act of the free grace of God; it is the unconditional promise of blessing to be received by faith.

(c) But is it, then, quite unconditional? Is it not conditional upon faith? Here we open up a further stage of the argument. Every well-instructed Christian will agree that no one can claim rights against God on the ground of the "work of the law." But what about faith? Is not faith the indispensable condition? It is, says Paul, "those who are men of faith who are blessed with the faithful Abraham" (Gal. 3:9). Must we not say, then, that the blessings of the covenant are for those who have faith and that consequently those who do not have faith are excluded from the covenant? Are we not, therefore, back again with the idea of a privileged elite who can expect from God a blessing which the unbeliever cannot claim? Has not the doctrine of election led us inexorably back again into this morally intolerable cul-de-sac? And what is the good Christian to think when he sees the unbeliever, or the people of other faiths, showing evidence of the blessing of God as impressive as those to be seen in Christendom?

The crucial instance of unbelief, as far as the New Testament literature is concerned, is the fact that the majority of the people of Israel have not believed in Jesus. The unbelief of his own kinsmen is the source of Paul's deepest perplexity and anguish (Rom. 9:1–3). They *are* God's chosen, God's covenant people, God's beloved (9:4–5). Yet even in his covenant faithfulness God always retained his freedom — the sovereign freedom of the creator over his own works (9:6–29). In fact, Israel has been guilty of trying to turn the covenant into a contract, of trying to establish a claim upon God based upon their own fulfillment of the law (9:30–10:17). And therefore God has hardened their hearts. It is not that he has rejected them (unthinkable thought!) but that he has hardened them (10:18–11:10). Does that mean that, being unbelievers, they will be destroyed? Perish the thought! No! The purpose is that through their rejection of the gospel it may reach the Gentiles, and so they in turn will receive it back from the Gentiles (11:11–16). But this means that the Gentiles must equally recognize that they have no claim against God. The unbelief of the

Jews has created the possibility for Gentiles to be received
by a miracle of pure grace ("contrary to nature") into the
life of Israel. If they now begin to "boast over the branches"
— that is, to imagine that their faith gives them a claim
upon God which the unbelieving Jews do not have — then
they too will be cut off from the life of the true Israel
(11:17–24). Thus, though God's tactics may seem strange,
his strategy is clear. It is to destroy every claim in order to
leave the way clear for grace. It is to thwart every device for
turning the covenant into a contract. It is "to consign all
men to disobedience that he may have mercy upon all."
Thus the unbelief of Israel does not mean their final rejection; it is part of God's wonderful strategy. The purpose is
both that "the full number of the Gentiles [shall] come in"
and that "all Israel shall be saved" (11:25–32). This salvation can only be in mutual dependence and relatedness. As I
said earlier, the corporate nature of the salvation which God
purposes is a necessary part of the divine purpose of salvation according to the biblical view that no one could receive
it as a direct revelation from above but only through the
neighbor, only as part of an action in which he opens his
door and invites his neighbor to come in. The reader might
have objected that there was a flaw in the argument, for
whereas "the nations" could only receive salvation through
Israel, the elect nation, Israel itself would apparently receive the gift directly "from above," and not from the
neighbor. But in fact, says Paul, Israel will receive the gift of
salvation only by opening her doors to the "heathen."

It is here in this argument of Romans 9–11 that the
inner consistency of the biblical doctrine of election becomes most clear. There is no salvation except in a mutual
relatedness which reflects that eternal relatedness-in-love
which is the being of the triune God. Therefore salvation
can only be by the way of election: one must be chosen and
called and sent with the word of salvation to the other. But
therefore also the elect can receive the gift of salvation only
through those who are not the elect. The purpose of God's
action for salvation in Christ is nothing other than the

completing of his purpose of creation in Christ. It has in view, not "the soul" conceived as an independent monad detached from other souls and from the created world, but the human person knit together with other persons in a shared participation in and responsibility for God's created world.

*　*　*　*　*

To summarize what has been said so far in this chapter, we have found in the biblical teaching about election the clue to the problem of the relation between the cosmic universality of the kingdom of God which we proclaim and the particularity of the history with which we are concerned: Israel among all the nations, Jesus among all the religious leaders of world history, Christianity among all the religions. But we have seen that the doctrine of election has to be guarded against perversion in three ways — ways which represent three degrees of subtlety.

(*i*) At the simplest level we have to guard against the perversion which regards election as the conferring of a privileged status. This is the perversion against which the prophets of Israel constantly had to fight, and we have to fight it in the Christian church.

(*ii*) At a more subtle level there is the perversion which turns the covenant into a contract, so that those who keep the law are entitled to claim the blessing promised in the covenant. This was the issue in the conflict between Paul and the Judaizers.

(*iii*) At a still more subtle level is the perversion which, starting from the true statement that God's promise is to be received by faith, converts faith into a ground upon which we can make claims upon God's blessing over against the unbelievers. This is the issue in Paul's argument of Romans 9–11, where he has to warn the believing Gentiles that they must not boast over the unbelieving Jews, for God's purpose is to save both the Gentiles and "all Israel." Even the unbelief of the Jews is taken up into God's strategy of grace. Among the Jews there is a believing minority "chosen by grace" (11:5), and the unbelief of the majority is the means God uses, not for their destruction, but for their ultimate salvation through the witness of the believing Gentiles (11:11–12).

II

At this point in the argument two questions press for an answer, and we must deal with them before going further. Briefly stated they are as follows:

1. The exposition given so far of the doctrine of election may seem to lead straight to universalism, that is, to the doctrine that there can be no possibility of final exclusion from God's salvation.

2. The exposition has taken for granted the biblical picture of world history as centered in a series of "acts of God," among which his act of choosing, calling, and sending a people to be the bearers of his universal purpose of blessing has the central place. How can such a view of world history be sustained in the face of the picture of the history of the world produced by the work of modern historical science?

1. There can be no doubt that just as the perspective of the Bible is the whole history of humanity and of the cosmos, so also it is full of what one may call universalist overtones. The primal covenant with Noah is an unconditional promise of blessing for the whole human race. The covenant with Abraham looks to the blessing of all the nations. In the New Testament Paul, as we have seen, thinks of "all Israel" and "the fullness of the Gentiles" being gathered into Christ's salvation. In one of the passages where he draws a parallel between Adam and Christ he writes: "As one man's trespass led to condemnation for all men, so one man's act of righteousness leads to acquittal and life for all men" (Rom. 5:18). The salvation we share in Christ seems to be as universal as the sin we share in Adam. The fourth Gospel speaks of Jesus drawing "all men" to himself (John 12:32) and of his taking away the sin of the world (John 1:29).

On the other hand there are equally clear and much

more numerous passages, especially in the New Testament, which speak of a coming judgment and of the possibility of being rejected. Nothing could exceed the gravity and solemnity of the warnings about this which are given in the teachings of Jesus and Paul. All the strands of tradition which are woven together in the New Testament bear witness to this. We would part company with the New Testament altogether if we ignored it.

I believe it is essential to hold firmly together both the universalist perspective of the Bible and the clear teaching about judgment and the possibility of rejection. Let me try to spell out in detail what I believe this involves.

(a) We must reject the kind of rationalistic universalism which argues from the omnipotence of God's love to the necessary ultimate salvation of every soul. The very easiness of this syllogism ought to warn us against it. It does not give serious attention to the freedom and responsibility which God has given to the human person. It moves in a different world of thought from that of the Bible.

(b) We must refuse to engage in speculation about the ultimate salvation of other people. In the many references to final judgment in the teaching of Jesus, the most characteristic feature is the emphasis on the element of surprise. Normal expectations will be proved completely wrong. Those who were sure of their acceptance will find themselves rejected. The last will be first and the first, last. The righteous will be shocked by the generosity of the Lord to other people (Matt. 20:1–16) and by his severity to themselves (Matt. 7:21–23). Therefore we are warned not to take upon ourselves the judgment which is God's sole prerogative (Matt. 7:1–5). It is in line with this that when the disciples ask "Lord, will those who are saved be few?" Jesus swiftly replies with a direct warning to the questioners: "Strive to enter by the narrow door: for many, I tell you, will seek to enter and will not be able" (Luke 13:23–30). The question of eternal salvation and judgment is not for speculation about the fate of other people; it is an infinitely serious practical question addressed to me.

(c) A study of the very large number of references in the teaching of Jesus to the possibility of rejection at the final judgment shows that the prime target of his warning is precisely the people who are sure of their own salvation. It is directed not to the outsider but to the insider. It is those who say "Lord, Lord" who will find themselves rejected. It is the "sons of the kingdom" who will be cast out. It is the branches of the vine which will be cut off and burned if they do not bear fruit. As always in the Bible, it is the elect who come under severe judgment. The one who is appointed steward is tempted to think he is master and so falls under judgment. Here we touch again the point which was discussed earlier: that God's saving purpose works by way of election means that those who are chosen and called fall into the temptation of imagining that they have a claim on God which others do not. God must destroy this claim, for otherwise the sovereignty of grace will be undone. So the warnings of judgment are addressed primarily to the elect.

(d) At the risk of wearisome reiteration I must insist that the whole issue is misunderstood if it is argued in terms of the mathematical completeness of the number of the saved, conceiving them as an uncountable number of indi vidual souls. The universalism of the Bible will not be understood if we are thinking in terms of a multitude of spiritual monads and asking about the destiny of each one conceived as a separate individual. The universalism of the Bible consists in this: it shows us that God's saving purpose is addressed to the whole of his work in creation and to the human person, who has his real being only in his participation in this whole work. Salvation is a making whole and therefore it concerns the whole. This means, in terms of my own spiritual life: (1) I am never permitted to think of my own salvation apart from that of God's whole family and God's whole world; (2) at no point — not even at the point of death — am I permitted to turn my back upon my neighbors, upon that bit of the world's life in which I have shared, which I have tried to serve, and without which I would not be a human being at all; (3) the end to which I look, for which I long, and in which I will rejoice, is not that I am saved but that my Lord shall "see of the travail of his soul and be satisfied."

(e) But this biblical universalism is wholly compatible, and in fact requires, the acknowledgment that there remains the fearful possiblity of missing the mark, of falling short, of being rejected. There is a narrow path to be walked between two errors. On the one hand, the recognition of the possibility of rejection may lead into a self-centered anxiety and a drive to secure one's own personal destiny by a flurry of activity and piety. On the other hand, the assurance of God's grace may lead to a false sense of security, to that "hardening" of which Paul accuses the Jews. How does one find the true balance between a godly confidence in God's grace and a godly fear of God's judgment? The whole secret of the Christian life lies here, and Paul gives us a trustworthy clue to it in those passages where he likens the discipline of his life in Christ to the discipline of an athlete. Of his own ministry he says: "I pommel my body and subdue it, lest after preaching to others I myself should be disqualified" (I Cor. 9:27). And in the wonderful passage (Phil. 3) where he is thinking about his own life, its past, present, and future, he sees himself as an athlete in a race. He has not yet won the prize. It is before him. He presses on with both eagerness and confidence because Christ has already claimed him.

This is as far as possible from speculation about the question, "Are there few that will be saved?", from the kind of discussions about the possibilities of salvation for non-Christians, from the arguments about universalism which are common in some missionary discussions. The Bible is universalist in the sense that it is realistic about what human life really is — not the co-existence of a multitude of independent spiritual monads, but a participation with other human beings in a world which God has made, is making, and will make new. God's salvation is directed to these real human beings in this real world. But this universalism also takes absolutely seriously the freedom and re-

sponsibility which God has given to every human being, and
therefore it acknowledges the necessity of judgment and the
possibility of rejection. The Christian life is lived in the
life-giving tension between a godly fear and a godly
confidence.

2. We must now look at a second difficulty which besets
us in taking the doctrine of election as the clue to the
understanding of the role of mission in world history. We
have taken the Bible as our guide, and the Bible is essentially narrative in form. Its form is that of a universal history. It contains, indeed, much else — prayer, poetry, legis-
lation, ethical teaching, and so on. But essentially it is a
story. In our discussion hitherto we have relied uncritically
on this story. We have talked about acts of God in choosing,
calling, delivering, and sending his representatives to be the
bearers of his saving purpose. By what right do we talk in
this way, and how does this talk relate to the history of the
world (and of the eastern Mediterranean area) which we
read in the writings of secular historians?

(a) The world is, of course, full of stories. Many of them
are told over and over again. They appear in different forms
in different cultures. They are treasured, retold, and sometimes embroidered with additional detail, because they
"say" something which is true of human life always and
everywhere. In many cultures, not only in that of Israel, the
basic understanding of a people about "how things are" is
embodied in stories — stories about the creation of the
world, about the first human beings, stories of death and the
afterlife, stories of the struggle between good and bad in
human life.

What place should these stories have in our total understanding of how things are? One very influential way of
looking at them is to see them as varied illustrations of
truths which are eternal and universal. Their truth does not
lie in their "happenedness," in their accuracy as a record of
anything that really happened. Their truth is independent
of this; it is to be found in that which they point to and
illustrate and which can be verified now and always in

experience. The important thing is that "this is how things are," not that "this is what actually happened."

The philosophy of the Graeco-Roman world which has so much shaped our modern Western culture has predisposed us to look at these stories in this way. The truth about how things are is to be expressed in timeless statements. When we read that God is "infinite in being and perfection, a most pure spirit, invisible, without body, parts or passion, immutable, immense, eternal, incomprehensible, almighty, most wise, most holy, most free, most absolute" we recognize that we are in a world different from that of the Bible.[1] The Bible remains in the world of stories. Its God, in the famous words of Blaise Pascal, is not the God of the philosophers, but the God of Abraham, of Isaac, and of Jacob. The Bible does not tell stories which illustrate something true apart from the story. The Bible tells a story which is *the* story, the story of which our human life is a part. It is not that stories are part of human life, but that human life is part of a story. It is not that there are stories which illustrate "how things are"; it is that we do not begin to understand how things are unless we understand how they were and how they will be. Our so-called eternal truths are the attempts we make at particular moments in the story to grasp and state how things are in terms of our experience at that point. They are all provisional and relative to time and place, as we recognize when as twentieth-century people we read the seventeenth-century language of the Westminster Confession. The reality with which we have to deal is the story — the story which begins before the creation of the world, ends beyond the end of the world, and leads through the narrow road that is marked by the names of Abraham, Isaac and Jacob, Moses, Amos, Paul, and, name above every name, the name of Jesus.

(b) But this claim that we have in the Bible not just "stories" but "the story" brings us face to face with the questions raised by modern scientific historiography. There

---

1. Westminster Confession, II.1.

are other ways of telling the story of the world, and they do not find these names from one of the minor ethnic communities of the Near East in any way decisive for the history of the world. How is this biblical story related to "world history" as it is understood in a modern school or university? There is a large literature on this question which is perhaps the most important issue in the dialogue between the gospel and the contemporary culture of the Western world. (If this book were being written in a different cultural context one could best discuss this question in the section on the gospel and the cultures of mankind, for the "modern scientific historiography" of which we speak is a product of a particular culture and is by no means to be seen as something universal. Writing in the present context, however, the question must be faced at this point.)

Modern scientific historiography involves asking such questions as the following about all the stories which are told. What is the source of the story? Does it come from eyewitnesses or at secondhand? What evidence is there about the credibility of those who saw, reported, or retold the story? What was their purpose in telling the story? To whom were they telling it? What interests and influences would be likely to shape their telling? What collateral information do we have from other sources which bears on these events? For the asking of these and similar questions historians are continually sharpening their tools and accumulating and organizing more information bearing on the story.

But all these tools are handled and this information is arranged by a human being whose work is also shaped by the interests and influences of his time and place and culture. The directions in which he decides to probe, the questions he asks, the weight he gives to different witnesses and different types of evidence, the analogies by means of which he tries to understand the events and characters reported, the models by means of which he organizes his material — all are shaped by the culture of which he is a part, by the experiences, hopes, and fears of that part of the whole fabric of human society in which he has his place. It is obviously as true of the work of the historian as it is of every kind of study that we can only understand anything by relating it to the experience we already have. The language we use, the models and analogies without which we cannot make sense of a mass of information, are all furnished in the first instance by our culture and shaped by the experiences of our time and place. History has to be continually rewritten because, in the words of E. H. Carr, history is a continuing conversation between the present and the past.

(c) The data of the historian are records of happenings which were recorded because they were significant for someone. The historian in his turn selects a tiny fragment of all this material on the basis of what is significant to him. But how does one decide what is significant? If one is writing the history of a relatively small institution such as a school or college the problem may not be very difficult. The volume of recorded happenings is small. Everything that has been significant in the life of the college can be told within one volume. But how does one decide what is significant? He decides only on the basis of a view, implied or explicit, about what *has* been significant — the life of the nation of which the college is a part. And to ask this question is to be led on to the wider question of the role of the nation in the life of the whole human society. What events are significant for human history as a whole? One cannot answer that question without some idea, if only a provisional one, about the shape of the human story as a whole. And our ideas about this are shaped by our cultures. A "history of the world" written in Oxford will be very different from one written in Warsaw, in Peking, or in Madras. The same recorded facts are equally available to all, but the selection, organization, and interpretation will be different because the whole human situation is understood differently.

No one can tell a story well unless he has seen the meaning of it, unless he has "seen the point." Normally the point is clear only at the end. Our difficulty is that we are still in the middle of the story: we can investigate the past, but the future is hidden and we do not know the end. Our different ways of writing history, our different pictures of the story, are our ways of expressing our different beliefs about its end. We could amend E. H. Carr's sentence to read: History is a continuing conversation between the present and the past about the future.

Since the future is hidden from us, how can there be a universal history — a picture of the whole story which is equally valid in Oxford, Warsaw, Peking, or Madras? How can the real significance of any event anywhere be understood in a way which is valid for all? It can happen only if the point of the story has been revealed even before the story has come to its end.

(d) I have deliberately used the word "revealed" because at this point we cannot avoid the concept of revelation. Such concepts as "research," "study," and "observation" are irrelevant at this point. No amount of research will enable us to see the point of a story before the story is finished. The inductive method, which begins by examining all the data, is here futile. A very simple parable will illustrate the point. If you come across a building site where work is going on, and if you wish to know what is being built and for what purpose, it will not be possible to satisfy your curiosity by measuring the holes in the ground and examining the building material which is being assembled. You cannot know what is going on, much less make intelligent proposals for action, unless you have been told whether it is to be a private house, or an office, or a factory. The architect must tell you; the end product is still in his mind and on his drawing board. You can learn his plans only by receiving what he has to tell. At this point the concept of revelation is not an alien intrusion into the process of responsible human knowing. There is no other possibility.

Within the Christian tradition the Bible is received as the testimony to those events in which God has disclosed ("revealed") the shape of the story as a whole, because in Jesus the beginning and the end of the story, the Alpha and the Omega, are revealed, made known, disclosed. On the basis of this disclosure, therefore, it is possible to have a universal history, a way of understanding the whole story which is not determined by a starting point in the particular culture, time, and place where each of us stands. (I realize this statement immediately raises a whole range of new questions, for the Bible itself has its context in one particular cultural situation, and the Christian who confesses Christ as the meaning of history does so in a way which is conditioned by his culture. These questions will be dealt with in Chapter 9.) In fact, the idea of a universal history has come into our culture from the Bible. The great religions of Asia have not been interested in the construction of a universal history. All the religions which have their origin in the Indian subcontinent have seen the human story in terms of recurring cycles. The movement of time is interpreted on the basis of our experience of nature, which is the experience of continually repeated birth, growth, decay, death, and new birth. In Hindu thought the whole cosmos is involved in this cyclical movement. Each age (*kalpa*) of many millions of years comes to an end and is replaced by another. The story can never come to a point. There is no point in a circle, and so there is no story to tell. There are only stories.

(e) It appears to be only in those parts of the world where the faith of Israel has been at work that the idea of universal history has been present. In Europe since the time of the birth of the church the biblical picture of history has coexisted with and has often been overshadowed by the classical picture with its recurring cycles. Biblical language was bent into a cyclical shape, so that man's future was seen as a return to a past innocence — "Paradise Regained." But insofar as the European mind conceived of history as a meaningful story, the meaning was drawn from the Bible. In the eighteenth-century Enlightenment this biblical framework was gradually replaced by one which, continuing the biblical idea of an ongoing purpose and a real end of the human story, replaced God by man as the bearer of the meaning of history. The "Idea of Progress" was born. History was seen as the story of the progressive development of human knowledge and skill and the progressive achievement of man's mastery over nature and his emancipation from bondage to ancient tradition and custom. The man of the Enlightenment, modern western European man living in the Age of Reason, was the leader of human progress. The meaning of the story as a whole was to be found in the progressive victory of human science and skill, informed and guided by reason, over all the ancient traditions and dogmas by which men had been, and still were, fettered.

It is obvious that if universal history is understood from this point of view, the story the Bible tells has to be reinterpreted. It becomes part of that sector of human affairs which is called "religion." Insofar as "religion" is still recognized as a significant human activity (albeit one which belongs to the private rather than the public sector), the stories about Abraham, Moses, and Jesus will have an important place in the "religious instruction" period of a school curriculum. But in the class period devoted to world history they will have a much less important place than, for example, the development of Greek science and philosophy, Roman law and political organization, or modern technology. Inevitably also, as has been taking place ever since the eighteenth century, the Bible narrative itself will be reinterpreted. The models and analogies proved by the modern scientific world view will be used to reinterpret the historical evidence available in the Bible and other ancient records. The Christ of faith — Jesus as he has been interpreted and understood within the tradition which has accepted the Bible story as the "real" story of man — will be set aside, and the search will be made for the Jesus of history — Jesus as he can be interpreted and understood within the axioms and models furnished by the post-Enlightenment understanding of the human story.

(f) We are now in a position to attempt a direct answer to the question about the relation of the biblical "story" of God's dealing with man by the way of election to the story of mankind as it is told in a modern history of the world. The biblical story is not a separate story. It is not a special history ("salvation history") apart from human history as a whole. The whole story of mankind is one single fabric of interconnected events, and the story the Bible tells is part of it. The study of the Old Testament runs out into and draws upon the work of archaeologists and historians working on the early civilizations of Mesopotamia, Palestine, and Egypt. The study of the New Testament cannot be done in isolation from the work of secular historians of first-century religion, politics, and culture in the eastern Roman Empire and from such discoveries as have been made through the finding of the Dead Sea Scrolls. No fence can be erected around the biblical story; it is part of the human story ("The Word was made *flesh*"). Therefore it is and must be open to all the critical probing of the historian. The scholar must be and is free to test every part of the ground and to use all the skills which the modern study of history has developed. If, in the supposed interests of faith, we try to keep the critic out, we are in effect denying the historicity of the story and turning the gospel into a myth. The historical scholar must come in with all his tools.

The debate begins when we ask not about his tools, but about his presuppositions, axioms, models, analogies, and paradigms. Naturally he will bring these with him. He cannot do otherwise. As I have said before, none of us can begin to understand anything except by relating it to what he already knows, and therefore to the models by which he has hitherto organized his experience. The devout Hindu comes to the biblical story and does not find it difficult to interpret Jesus in terms of his concept of a *jeevanmukta*. His "life of Jesus" will be constructed by organizing the material around this concept. A Marxist who studies the Gospels will form his picture of Jesus on the basis of his fundamental understanding of the forces which shape human life. The Western academic whose basic axioms and models have been shaped by the development of European thought in the past two hundred years will likewise interpret Jesus in terms of those models. This, he will be convinced, is the "real" Jesus of history, as contrasted with the Jesus of traditional Christian dogma. The Christian believer looks at the same data, but he brings to the interpretation of them the presupposition that the point of the whole human story has been revealed here; that in Jesus the whole meaning of the story is disclosed; that everything else, including all the axioms and presuppositions and models developed in all the cultures of mankind are relativized by and must be judged in the light of this presupposition. And the presupposition is the one which has shaped and has been borne by the believing community which is the church, from the first disciples to this day. This is expressed in the great credal affirmations which the church has used through the centuries. It is from within these presuppositions that the Christian seeks to understand the biblical story. The biblical story is not a separate story: it is part of the unbroken fabric of world history. The Christian faith is that this is the place in the whole fabric where its pattern has been disclosed, even though the weaving is not yet finished. Christian faith is thus a way of understanding world history which challenges and relativizes all other models by which the meaning of history is interpreted.

(g) As soon as these words are written a host of questions arise. Every Christian is both a member of the universal church and also a participant in a particular culture. There is not one Christian interpretation of Jesus: there are many different ones, shaped by different cultures. The church itself is a changing reality, and its confession of the faith has changed and must continue to change. Within the New Testament itself there is not one single "model" for interpreting Jesus. All these things are true, and we must consider their bearing on our main theme in a later chapter (Chapter 9). Here I must try only to summarize what has been said up to this point about the relation between the biblical story with its center in the history of God's election and the story of mankind as it is told by the secular historian.

(*i*) The Christian's confession is the confession of a faith regarding the meaning and end of the human story as a whole. This confession compels him to challenge every understanding of the human story which looks to an end other than that which is disclosed in Jesus.

(*ii*) Believing that the biblical story is part of the whole history of which his life is a part, the Christian refuses to allow the biblical story to be excluded from the critical questions which are properly put to all historical records. It is essential for him to know "what really happened." But he will also be ready to explore and question the hidden presuppositions which underlie every exercise in historical enquiry.

(*iii*) The presuppositions with which the Christian comes to the biblical story are those which have shaped the community of believers from the first disciple onwards. The Christian draws these presuppositions from his sharing in the life, worship, and obedience of the community. It is of the essence of this community that in it people of many different cultures, times, and human situations are, in spite of their differences, united in the confession of Jesus as Alpha and Omega.

(*iv*) Since the Christian faith is a faith regarding the meaning and end of the human story as a whole, this faith cannot be confessed except in the context of the actual secular history of the present hour. To be specific, this must mean a provisional interpretation of the meaning of contemporary secular events (discerning the signs of the times) and concrete action in the various sectors of secular life directed towards the true end for which God has created humanity and the world (Christian obedience in the common life). In other words, the question of the relation of the biblical story to the whole "story of mankind" is a question which has to be answered in action. The Christian confession about the meaning and end of history can make good its claim to truth over against other interpretations of human history only through actions in which this confession is embodied in deed — and in suffering. If the Christian confession is true, the Acts of God do not cease with the Acts of Apostles.

We have now, therefore, to go on to ask: What are the actions by which the believing community will fulfill God's purpose for it as the community chosen, called, and sent with a view to the salvation of the world?

8

Mission as Action for God's Justice

I HAVE TRIED to describe mission in terms of the proclamation, the presence, and the prevenience of the reign of
God. That reign concerns the whole history of the human
family and of the cosmos. At the heart of the prayer Jesus
taught his disciples is the petition: "Thy will be done on
earth as in heaven." God's will is to be done on earth. The call
of Jesus to believe the good news of the impending kingdom
leads at once to the call "Follow me." There can be no
separation between believing and following, between faith
and obedience. The prayer "Thy will be done" is in vain if it
is not made visible in action for the doing of that will.
Consequently, missions have never been able to separate the
preaching of the gospel from action for God's justice.

They have sometimes tried to do so. One can tell the
story of missionaries who have set out with the firm deter-
mination to do nothing except preach the gospel, to be pure
evangelists uninvolved in all the business of "social service." But the logic of the gospel has always been too strong
for them. A hungry man comes asking for food; shall he be
refused in the name of the gospel? A sick child is brought
for help. There are children all around with no opportunity
for schooling. And so the missionary has been drawn, in
spite of his pure theology, into the work of education, healing, social service, "agricultural missions," and a host of

102

similar activities. Out of such small beginnings has grown the vast network of services which has provided the foundation for modern education and medicine throughout most of Asia, Africa, and Latin America, as well as for many of the new crops and agricultural methods upon which whole populations now depend.

And yet there has always been an undertone of questioning about all this activity, even something of a bad conscience about it. Over and over again it has been urged that all this "social service" deflects the attention of missions from the primary business of evangelism. New agencies have been formed vowing to avoid all this entanglement in secular affairs and to concentrate entirely on the preaching of the gospel. But again and again the simple logic of the gospel itself has drawn them irresistibly into some work of education, healing the sick, feeding the hungry, helping the helpless.

Various arguments have been deployed in the attempt to justify these activities as part of the work of missions. They have been defended as a way of gaining a hearing for the gospel in quarters where there is resistance to direct preaching. They have been defended as a means of building up a strong indigenous church which will itself evangelize its own nation. Thus the enterprise of Christian higher education in India, originally understood as a method of evangelism, was defended in the Lindsay Commission Report of 1931 primarily as a way of training leadership for the Indian church. In the period following the First World War it was common to describe these activities as part of the "larger evangelism." One of the most popular missionary texts of the period was the words of Jesus, "I came that they may have life, and have it abundantly" (John 10:10), and "abundant life" was interpreted as the abundance of the good things that modern education, healing, and agriculture would provide for the deprived peoples of the world.

It is obvious that this whole discussion which has been so prominent in the missionary thinking of the past hundred years has presupposed the colonial situation. Missions came from the colonizing powers to areas which were less advanced economically and technically than the "home" countries. Quite apart from all other arguments, simple compassion called for the sharing of the good things of life. Missionaries in this situation had problems which did not trouble Paul in the first century or even Robert de Nobili in the sixteenth. In both these cases the missionary was going to a culture which was as advanced as or more advanced than his own. Paul was under no obligation of compassion to offer educational or medical services to the people of Ephesus or Corinth! The "signs and wonders" which were part of his work as a missionary (Rom. 15:19) carried no colonial overtones.

This part of the work of missions during the colonial period was continued during the period of the dismantling of the colonial empires under such names as "technical assistance" and, later, "development." The governments and other secular and ecclesiastical agencies in the Western nations built upon and greatly enlarged the work which missions had been doing to provide schools, hospitals, and technical services, to improve farming methods, and to develop new industries. The basic pattern was still that of the colonial period. The prevalent values were those of the Western nations. The world was divided into "developed" and "undeveloped," "underdeveloped," or "developing" nations. Whatever terms were used, the underlying concept was that "development" means moving in the direction taken by the West European and North American peoples and that the social and cultural values which had in the past governed people's thinking in Asia and Africa were to be replaced by those which have governed the Western nations in the two centuries since the Enlightenment.

It is obvious that the whole group of ideas and practices which are focused in the word "development" can only represent a transitional phase. In the first place, even if one could for the moment accept the idea that the values which have governed the evolution of Western societies in the past two hundred years are the proper ones for all mankind to follow, it is morally unacceptable that "development," so understood, should be a process controlled and directed by the rich countries. The people of the world will not permanently accept a situation in which a rich minority determines what and how much knowledge, healing, and skill shall be made available to the rest. In the second place, and more fundamentally, it is by no means self-evident that the rest of the world will or should develop the kind of society which has been developed in Europe and North America during the past two hundred years. The model within which both the "service" activities of missions and the "development" activities of governments have operated during the past hundred and fifty years is no longer acceptable. As far as the missionary thinking of the churches is concerned, one can record a strong movement in the last ten years (1968–78) away from the idea of service offered by the strong to the weak, towards actions designed to enable the needy and powerless to become aware of their situation, to understand the forces which control and dominate them, and to organize themselves for their own liberation. A very important part in this movement has been played by the techniques of "conscientization" developed by the Brazilian educator, Paulo Freire. For Freire, all education is either for domination or for liberation. Much of the education offered in the past by mission schools and colleges has been designed to hide from its victims the real nature of the forces which control them and to condition them to accept their own powerlessness. What is required is a kind of education which awakens the consciousness of the oppressed to the reality of their oppression and liberates them to become the authors of their own freedom.

This has already brought us to the third factor which renders the concept of "development" inoperative. The Marxist analysis of the working of the free market system has gained increasing acceptance even among those who do not accept the Marxist doctrines of man and of history. It has become evident to more and more people that "development" and "underdevelopment" are two sides of the same coin, that in fact the nations are locked in an economic system which functions inexorably in such a way as to make the rich richer and the poor poorer. It has been frequently pointed out that the gap between rich and poor nations was wider at the end of the "development decade" than at its beginning. In the new economic circumstances which followed the development of J. M. Keynes's theory of money and its international acceptance at the Bretton Woods meeting, the free market economy had an immense new lease on life. The twenty-five years following the end of the Second World War witnessed a growth of the world economy quite unprecedented in human history. Among the main organs of growth were the transnational corporations, many of which commanded larger resources than the majority of sovereign states. No political machinery existed at the world level which could exercise the kind of controls over the working of the free market system which are operated by all national governments to mitigate the effects of its working within their own nations. In this situation the Marxist analysis of the working of the free market economy has gained a new credibility. More and more people who do not accept the total Marxist view of human nature and destiny have become convinced that the Marxist economic analysis is true, and the model in terms of which they view the problems of world poverty is no longer that of "developed" and "developing" nations, but that of "oppressors" and "oppressed," "exploiters" and "exploited." The action which is called for by Christians is thus seen, not in terms of "development aid," but in terms of revolutionary action for the liberation of the victims of oppression.

I

The discussion about the role of "service" in the missionary work of the church is thus now replaced by a new discussion. We are no longer thinking about "services" such as have been traditionally offered by the (Christian) rich to the (pagan) poor in the form of schools, hospitals, and agricultural projects. We have now to listen to the missiology formulated within the consciousness of the Christian who is part of the poor world, a missiology centered in the demand for liberation in the name of God's justice. It is in these terms that we must face in our day the question of the relation between the preaching of the gospel and action for God's justice as part of the church's mission. Does the "story" which runs through Abraham and Moses to Jesus and from Jesus and Paul and the church to us here and now run on into action for revolution? Is this what "salvation history" means now?

The "theology of liberation" accepts as the fundamental starting point that there are not two histories, sacred and profane, but only one, and that "the history of salvation is the very heart of human history."[1] From this it goes on to insist that there can be no dualism between a timeless "spiritual" truth and the time-conditioned concrete historical situation. Therefore true theology does not begin in the realm of ideas. It begins with praxis. As Miguez Bonino says:

> It is not merely that theology is at the service of action, as in a way it was in the old Jesuit order: seeing, judging, acting. Rather action is itself the truth. Truth is at the level of history, not in the realm of ideas. Reflection on praxis, on human significant action, can only be authentic when it is done from within, in the vicinity of the strategic and tactical plane of human action.[2]

And again, as the same writer puts it still more clearly, "There is no truth outside or beyond the concrete historical events in which men are involved as agents."[3]

Liberation theology rejects the idea that truth is a timeless spiritual entity which, so to say, floats above the moving current of history. Salvation is God's action in history, and

---

1. Gustavo Gutierrez, *Theology of Liberation* (Maryknoll, N.Y.: Orbis Books, 1973), p. 153.
2. Miguez Bonino, *Revolutionary Theology Comes of Age* (London: SPCK, 1975), p. 72.
3. Ibid., p. 88.

therefore truth can only be known through participation in this action. In this insistence liberation theology is keeping much closer to the Bible than is the theology which uses the concepts of idealistic philosophy. In the Old Testament the primary model of salvation is provided by the exodus from Egypt. Indeed, this is much more than a model: it is God's supreme saving action. God's revelation of himself to Moses is in the form of a call to go and liberate captive Israel. God makes himself known as the Liberator God. God's cause and the cause of those exploited immigrant workers are the same. The exodus from Egypt and the deliverance from Pharaoh's pursuing army are not described in the record as signs or even as illustrations of God's saving work. Instead, there is a simple identification: this deliverance *is* God's salvation (Ex. 14:13; 15:2). Yahweh is forever afterwards identified as the one "who brought you up out of the land of Egypt, out of the house of bondage." There is no question here of an ideal of justice which stands above both Moses and Pharaoh and to which each makes his own application for his particular case, on the basis of which there could be some sort of compromise solution between the two parties. No, God is on the side of the slaves, and their oppressors are God's enemies. There is no superior position from which a neutral arbitrator could decide between them.

The theologians of liberation in Latin America see their situation in these terms. God's cause is the cause of the exploited peasants and miners. The landowners, the mine owners, the transnational corporations who exploit them for their own profit — all are God's enemies. The church, if it is truly the church of God, can be on one side only. The idea that the church can be a neutral arbitrator, a reconciler between the conflicting parties, or the exponent of a "third way" between active revolt and passive submission, is an illusion, a part of the false ideology which is used by the exploiting class to maintain its power over the exploited. Any talk of salvation apart from action for the liberation of the exploited is false. It is part of a false theology which is determined by an idealist philosophy and not by the revelation of God as he is in the Bible. Wherever we look in the Old Testament we find that the prophets and psalmists speak of salvation in terms of actual historic happenings: deliverance from famine, sickness, danger, enemies, and oppression. Therefore, for the biblical writers, to "know the Lord" is not a matter of intellectual contemplation or mystical union; it is a matter of doing justice and mercy in concrete situations. When Jeremiah comments sarcastically on the king's building program, he contrasts the king's conduct with that of the king's father and says: " 'He [the father] judged the cause of the poor and needy; then it was well. Is not this to know me? says the Lord' " (Jer. 22:16). Those who claim to know the Lord but do evil are deceived. They are far from God. And the same teaching is given in the New Testament. There is no knowledge of God apart from the love of God, and there is no love of God apart from the love of the neighbor. "He who does not love does not know God" (I John 4:8; cf. 3:14–24).

Love and justice are distinct concepts, but where justice is denied love is certainly denied. If the economic order is such that the owners of land and capital can and do exploit and oppress the workers, then the commandment of love must mean more than marginal acts of personal charity; it must mean action to end exploitation. It must mean actions for liberation of which the Exodus is the model, and this must mean taking the side of the exploited and fighting against the exploiter. Fundamental to the theology of liberation is the refusal to allow a separation between truth and action. Christians who are products of the idealist tradition in Western Christendom will reason somewhat as follows: "There is a truth — the truth of the gospel — which I can learn and know. After that, as a second step, I have to decide how to apply that truth to my situation. I realize that different Christians will apply the gospel truth in different ways. Our judgments are fallible. The gospel is one, but the applications will differ." To this the liberation theologian says

"No!" Action is itself the truth."[4] You cannot know the truth except by doing the truth, and that means action for the liberation of the oppressed. God was known to Moses only in and through his acceptance of God's call to go and confront Pharaoh with the demand that the slaves be set free.

The Exodus is the central paradigm for liberation in the thought of the theologians we are considering. How are we to relate the Exodus story to the events which form the center of the Christian story — the events of the incarnation, cross, and resurrection? Christians have always seen the events of the Exodus as prefiguring the work of Christ. This goes back at least as far as the writings of Paul and is embodied in the tradition which lies behind all four Gospels — the relation between the death of Jesus and the Passover. But how are these two stories related? The relation has often been conceived in terms of a spiritualizing or allegorizing of the Exodus story. In this tradition the Exodus is seen as a sort of parable of the inward and spiritual liberation which Christ has accomplished in his cross. But this is to fall back again into the dualism which the Bible consistently denies between man's outward and his inward life — a dualism which, needless to say, is absolutely rejected by liberation theology.

Some theologians have tried to make the connection by making Jesus into a political revolutionary. Elaborate efforts have been made to prove that Jesus was really part of the Zealot movement — the "freedom fighters" of his time. It is certainly clear from the record that the death of Jesus was a profoundly political happening. This is brought out with special clarity in the fourth Gospel. That the notice of his charge, fastened to the cross, read "Jesus of Nazareth, King of the Jews" makes it clear that there were profound political implications in the trial and execution. However, careful scholarship cannot corroborate the claim that Jesus identified himself with the Zealot movement. Indeed, it is dif-

---

4. Ibid., p. 72.

ficult to see what conclusions one would draw if it could be proved that he did. In terms of *realpolitik* the Zealots were a disaster for the cause of Israel, and if Jesus was a Zealot we seem to have the best possible reason for forgetting him altogether.

A much wiser and more biblical way of relating the two stories is given by one of the major theologians of liberation. Gustavo Gutierrez distinguishes three senses in which we can speak of liberation. First is *political* liberation, in which the emphasis is on the conflict between the oppressor and the oppressed. Second is the concept of liberation as the continuous process by which man throughout history is assuming conscious responsibility for his own destiny; one might speak of this as the *cultural* aspect of liberation. Third, one must speak of *spiritual* liberation through Christ — liberation from sin and restoration to fellowship with God.

These three levels mutually affect each other, but they are not the same. One is not present without the others, but they are distinct: they are all part of a single, all-encompassing salvific process, but they are to be found at different levels. Not only is the growth of the Kingdom not reduced to temporal progress; because of the Word accepted in faith, we see that the fundamental obstacle to the Kingdom, which is sin, is also the root of all misery and injustice; we see that the very meaning of the growth of the Kingdom is also the ultimate precondition for a just society and a new man. One reaches this root and this ultimate precondition only through the acceptance of the liberating gift of Christ, which surpasses all expectations. But, inversely, all struggle against exploitation and alienation, in a history which is fundamentally one, is an attempt to vanquish selfishness, the negation of love. This is the reason why any effort to build a just society is liberating. And it has an indirect but effective impact on the fundamental alienation. It is a salvific work, although it is not all of salvation. As a human work it is not exempt from ambiguities, any more than what is considered to be strictly "religious" work. But this does not weaken its basic orientation nor its objective results.

Temporal progress — or, to avoid this aseptic term, the liberation of man — and the growth of the Kingdom are both directed toward complete communion of men with God and of men among themselves. They have the same goal, but they do not follow parallel roads, not even convergent ones. The growth of the Kingdom is a process which occurs historically *in* liberation, insofar as liberation means a greater fulfilment of man. Liberation is a precondition for the new society, but this is not all it is. While liberation is implemented in liberating historical events, it also denounces their limitations and ambiguities, proclaims their fulfilment, and impels them effectively towards total communion. This is not an identification. Without liberating historical events, there would be no growth of the Kingdom. But the process of liberation will not have conquered the very roots of oppression and the exploitation of man by man without the coming of the Kingdom, which is above all a gift. Moreover, we can say that the historical, political liberating event *is* the growth of the Kingdom and *is* a salvific event; but it is not *the* coming of the Kingdom, not *all* of salvation. It is the historical realization of the Kingdom and, therefore, it also proclaims its fullness. This is where the difference lies. It is a distinction made from a dynamic viewpoint, which has nothing to do with the one which holds for the existence of two juxtaposed "orders," closely connected or convergent, but deep down different from each other.[5]

Negatively, then, the Exodus story is not to be regarded simply as an allegory of a purely personal and spiritual liberation accomplished in Christ; nor is the work of Christ to be regarded simply as a further example (this time unsuccessful!) of the sort of political liberation described in the book of Exodus. Rather, acts of political (and cultural) liberation in history are signs which point towards the fullness of liberation because and insofar as they themselves share the character of liberation. They partake of the nature of salvation, but they are not the whole of salvation.

This is a much more satisfactory position than either of the two which are denied. But we may question whether it really does justice to all the facts. The difficulty which I feel about it becomes very explicit in the text which Gutierrez quotes as the summary of this part of his argument:

All the dynamism of the cosmos and of human history, the movement towards the creation of a more just and fraternal

5. Gutierrez, *Theology of Liberation*, pp. 176–177.

world, the overcoming of social inequalities among men, the efforts, so urgently needed on our continent, to liberate man from all that depersonalizes him — physical and moral misery, ignorance, and hunger — as well as the awareness of human dignity (*Gaudium et spes,* no. 22), all these originate, are transformed, and reach their perfection in the saving work of Christ. In him and through him salvation is present at the heart of man's history, and there is no human act which, in the last instance, is not defined in terms of it.[6]

This eloquent passage, which suggests the thought of Teilhard de Chardin, evokes a picture of human history which is more optimistic and much less ambiguous than the picture suggested in the New Testament. In what way, exactly, does "all the dynamism of . . . human history" reach its perfection in the saving work of Christ? How does one interpret the cross in relation to the (perfectly legitimate) aspirations of the Jews of Jesus' time for political liberation? How does one interpret the apocalyptic terms in which the New Testament speaks about the history which is still to be enacted? Does the picture which is here given enable us to find in practice the right path to walk between the longing that every person should come to know Jesus as his personal Savior and the longing that every person should enjoy the political and cultural freedom which are proper to human dignity? I have drawn attention to the fact that missions have always been drawn by an apparently irresistible logic into secular forms of service such as education, healing, social service, and the development of agriculture and industry, and to the fact that at the same time they have constantly developed a bad conscience about their service. Is this bad conscience to be regarded simply as the result of a wrong theology? It is fairly easy to speak of a "holistic evangelism" which looks both to the liberation of the person and to political and cultural liberation, but how do we hold these together in practice? It seems to me that a somewhat deeper questioning is needed.

---

6. *La Pastoral en las Misiones de America Latina,* p. 16, as quoted in Gutierrez, *Theology of Liberation,* p. 178.

The question I have to ask falls into two parts. The first concerns the eschatology implied in liberation theology and the second, its epistemology. Put in simpler terms, we are asking two questions: What is the end to which we look? and How do we know the direction?

II

Let me begin from the point at which I am in total agreement with the theologians of liberation, namely, in the rejection of the idealist view of man as essentially spiritual. Here we stand together in rejecting the dominant religious traditions of mankind. Our own Western culture has never been able to hold to a biblical view of man except in an uneasy tension with the pagan view which we have inherited from the Greek and Roman elements in our history. The more ancient, more universal, and more "natural" view of man is being greatly strengthened in our day through the renewed contacts with Indian religion and culture. The relegation of religion to the private sector of human affairs which followed the stalemate in the religious wars of the seventeenth century makes it much easier for this view to be accepted as normal. In this view, "religion" concerns a particular aspect of man's life, namely, that which is private, personal, interior. It concerns his "soul." It looks for a "salvation" which is outside of history. From this point of view the events of political and cultural liberation are only significant insofar as they contribute to or hinder the development of the soul considered as a spiritual monad. In an extreme development of this view John Hick is prepared to conjure up out of his imagination a multitude of separate universes, each of which has no meaning except to provide opportunities for the evolution of these spiritual monads.[7]

In contrast to this ancient and dominant view, the Old Testament insists on seeing the human person as a single reality in whom body and soul are two aspects of one being.

---

7. John Hick, *Death and Eternal Life* (New York: Harper & Row, 1976).

In this view the story of humanity and of the world has a significance as a whole, and the life of each person is understood as part of the whole story. This corresponds to our experience of what it means to be human. We become and are human beings through our shared relationships with other human beings as part of the world of organic and inorganic matter. This is the real world which we know. We do not have knowledge of any other world, nor do we have experience of souls which have not become known to us as embodied persons. The Old Testament deals with human nature and destiny in this thoroughly realistic way. Why should there be any difficulty about accepting this? Why has this — which has so much common sense on its side — always remained a minority view as against the "spiritual" view of man?

The difficulty is that human experience constantly contradicts every claim that human life understood in this realistic sense has a significant future. The Old Testament hope in God's salvation falters and crumbles against the repeated triumphs of evil over good. Neither the exodus from Egypt nor the exodus from Babylon brings the final liberation. When and how are we to look for it? And what does liberation mean for those who have died in hope for it but without tasting it?

1. Death is the dark mystery which mocks any hope for a total liberation of man in history. I have emphasized the realism of the Old Testament understanding of human life. The only human life I know is the life I have received through my parents, which has been nurtured by all the influences of family, friends, teachers, and colleagues and which I now live as part of the common public life of the world and the shared life of family and friends and neighbors. This *is* human life. But it is not fully described by describing it in this way. I participate in this life as a subject who must accept responsibility for the way I see, listen, and understand and for the way I act. This is an unsharable responsibility. At the moment of decision I am alone. And I must make the decision in the knowledge that

at some point not known to me I shall be removed finally from this shared human life before it has reached the goal for which I long and strive. Even the small activities to which I have devoted myself will be left unfinished. Some small traces of what I have done may remain for a few years, but eventually all of it will be buried without a trace under the accumulating rubble of history.

This is the point at which a separation opens up between my life seen as part of the shared life of mankind and my life seen as the personal history which I alone experience from within and which no one else can experience with me. Death destroys the possibility of carrying through to the end the realistic, holistic view of man given in the Old Testament. It drives a wedge between the two ways of understanding my human life. I am tempted, almost driven into a choice between two ways of finding meaning for my life: to find it only in the future destiny of that subject which is myself, or to find it only in the future of the common human life in which I have shared.

The former choice is the one made in the main religious traditions of the world. The significance, the dignity, the ultimate meaningfulness of human life is secured by the faith that each human soul is offered the possibility of eternal security and joy in a world beyond and apart from the world of historical happenings. But this comfort is obtained at the cost of denying ultimate significance to the public history of which my life is a part. It provides, in the positive sense in which the phrase was originally meant, "opium for the people," an anodyne which can help men and women to endure the suffering of human life. But like all drugs it can be abused, as it has been constantly abused by those in power to prevent the suffering from becoming so unbearable that it erupts into revolution. Opium was administered where surgery was needed.

The second possibility has been most resolutely explored by Marxism. Marxism as an interpretation of history rests ultimately on the Old Testament vision of a meaningful future for the public life of humanity. It is a secularized version of the biblical hope. It achieves its consistency by resolutely turning aside from the other dimension of human experience. Significance is found only in the vision of a future age of freedom and justice for all; the life of the person who dies before the new age has come and who will never share in it has no significance in itself. The human person is simply part of the raw material to be used or discarded in the process of creating a new world. Stalinism is not an accidental outcome of Marxism: it is the logical development of it. The issue of human rights goes to the very roots of the Marxist ideology, as the leaders of the USSR rightly perceive. The struggle of our time for a new kind of socialism — "socialism with a human face" — is a struggle to reaffirm that other dimension of human existence which is denied when meaning is found only in the process of history. The unquenchable character of that longing for ultimate meaning for the human person is attested by the many affirmations of the Christian hope inscribed on the tombstones of Soviet heroes.

Is it, then, part of our human situation that we are trapped in a dilemma from which there is no escape: meaning for the human person at the cost of denying meaning for history, or meaning for history at the cost of denying meaning for the human person?

2. The gospel releases us from this dilemma because it deals with that which is its root. We have seen that it is the fact of death that drives a wedge between the two ways of understanding human life, the private and the public, the interior life of the person and the public life in which it shares. But death, in the perspective of the Bible, is a symptom of something deeper. It is, from one point of view, simply a biological fact, a necessary part of the cyclical process by which nature is continually renewed. But this purely naturalistic model does not enable us to understand our personal and public life as they really are. From the point of view of the human search for meaning, death is the negation of all meaning. It shears through the threads on the loom before the weaving is finished. It denies completion to

117

the pattern. It is the outward expression of the fact that all the patterns we are weaving are flawed, that all our achievements are ambiguous, and that none of them leads directly to the perfection we seek. Death, in the vivid language of the Bible, is the wages of sin. It is the outward sign of the fact that neither I nor my achievements are of themselves fit for the kingdom of God. The fact of death — my personal death, the deaths of those with whose lives mine has been intertwined, and the death of the plans I have made, the institutions I have served, and the civilization of which I am a part — cuts across the attractive picture of an unbroken ascent from the origins of the world to the final consummation of history. There is a chasm that cuts across the landscape between the place where I stand and the glorious vision of the holy city which I see on the horizon of my world. The path goes down into the chasm, and I do not see the bottom.

The gospel is good news because in Jesus Christ God has dealt with sin and death, has opened a way that goes down into that chasm and leads out into the uplands beyond it, and has thereby released me from the dilemma in which I was trapped. The life, death, and resurrection of Jesus have opened up a way on which I can travel towards the city knowing that the end of the journey will be a real consummation both of my personal history and of the public history in which I have shared. Jesus committed both himself and his cause completely into his Father's hands and went down the way that leads into the chasm: for himself, rejection, the cross, and death; for his cause, defeat and obliteration. In the resurrection God vindicated both him and his cause and gave to those who were willing to trust and follow him the assurance that the vision of the city is not a mirage. In the gift of the Spirit he gave them — while still *in via* — a foretaste of the life of the city. Trusting him, therefore, I can follow that way and lose myself in the service of God's cause, knowing that though I cannot create the city, God can raise up both me and my works, purged in the fire of judgment, to take a place in the life of the city. I am no longer in the dilemma between meaning for the personal life and meaning for the public life. I can live fully the life of a real person, part of the real world of society, history, and nature, and know that, because Christ is risen, my labor in the Lord is not futile (I Cor. 15:58).

One consequence of the powerful grip of a pagan religiosity on the mind of the Western culture which has had the Bible in its hands for so long is the fact that the resurrection of Jesus is constantly spoken of as if it had reference only to the individual human person. It has been treated as the ground of our hope for a personal future. It is this, but it is much more than this: it is the ground of our hope for a new world. Paul carefully spells out the implications of the resurrection. Christ is the "first fruits of those who are fallen asleep." But the harvest is not just "those who belong to Christ"; it is the destruction of all that opposes God's rule and the subjection of the whole cosmos to God (I Cor. 15:20–28).

For the fullest exposition of the unity of the Christian hope, embracing both the private and the public life of the human person, we turn to the eighth chapter of Romans. The exposition begins with the liberation which has already been accomplished. By giving his Son to die the death of sinful man, God delivered us from the grip of sin and death and placed us under a new jurisdiction — that of the Spirit. (As usual, Paul's fundamental affirmation is cast in a trinitarian form.) This is an accomplished liberation. Like all liberations it is a change of regime. The effect of the new regime of the Spirit is that God's will is done and God's gifts of life and peace are enjoyed (8:1–8).

The regime of the Spirit does not remain a purely inward and invisible thing: it works out in the renewal of the whole personality. As the resurrection of Jesus was not a merely "spiritual" event (using this adjective in its loose modern sense of "mental"), so the regime of the Spirit overcomes the dualism of body and spirit and extends to the renewal of the whole person (8:9–11).

The mark of this renewal will be, firstly, deliverance

119

from a servile religion to a filial religion, a religion of sonship; secondly, the presence of hope — because the son is also the heir; and thirdly, the acceptance of the vocation to share in the messianic sufferings through which alone Jesus has opened the way to glory (8:12–17).

This glory ("the glorious liberty of the children of God") and this suffering are part of the calling of the whole created world. The world is under the control of powers ("futilities"), but this is only in order to be released into the freedom of sonship (cf. Gal. 3:23–4:7). The pains of the world are the birth pangs of a new world, and the mark of the presence of the Spirit in us will be that we share in these pains as those who are full of hope — patient hope (8:18–25).

At the heart of this pain, where we do not even know how to pray, the Spirit is at work in our inarticulate groanings, which become part of his own beseeching. The agony of the world becomes, through the suffering and groaning of the church and through the work of the Spirit, part of the life of the triune God (8:26–27).

Corresponding to this inward working of the Spirit in the hearts of believers is the outward working of the Father, who orders all things in the cosmos towards the fulfillment of the purpose for which he has called them (8:28). This calling is based upon the predestinating grace of God who knew them before they were and will be faithful to them until the end, so that in all their tribulation they will be "more than conquerors" (8:29–39).

Here is a marvelously coherent and compelling picture of the participation of the church in world history. History is interpreted here as a struggle for liberation. The Christian has his place in it not just as a fighter for liberation but as one who has been liberated. Through the presence of the Spirit he is already a free person, bearing in his own life the freedom which belongs to the end. The community of those who follow Jesus is called to share in the struggle for liberation as those who are full of eager and patient hope: eager, because they have already tasted the freedom to which God calls all; patient, because God is to be trusted to complete that which he has begun.

3. Patience means suffering. It is in the measure that the church shares in the tribulation of the Messiah, in the conflict which occurs whenever the rule of God is challenged by other powers, that the church is also a bearer of hope.

This suffering is not the passive acceptance of evil; it is the primary form of witness against it. It is the way in which we follow Jesus along the way of the cross. Jesus challenged the power of evil consistently right to the end. At the very end, when the limit was reached, he surrendered, not to the power of evil, but into the hands of the Father. This final surrender is not defeat but victory. It is not opium, but is the victory by which the slain Lamb rules the cosmos. The church is enabled by the presence of the Spirit to share in that victory as it gives itself continually to be offered up in and through the Son to the Father. In this life the church is enabled to share in the victorious passion of the triune God.

There is both a faith that rebels and a faith that accepts, and they belong together. Jesus consistently attacked the power of evil. In no recorded case did he ever advise the handicapped and the sick to accept their lot; his unfailing response to their presence was to put forth his power to heal. He sent out his disciples with a commission to do the same. And yet he also told them that they must of necessity suffer, just as he would have to suffer. This paradox is at the very heart of the gospel. "He saved others; himself he cannot save." It belongs to the mission of the church to the end. The power given to the church to meet the power of evil is just the power to follow Jesus on the road that leads through suffering, through total surrender to the Father, to the gift of new life and a new world.

We are heirs with Christ of that new world, says Paul, "provided we suffer with him" (Rom. 8:17). The nature of that "suffering with" is compassion. In every human society so long as human beings are what we know them to be, there

121

will be unjust suffering. And even if we could expect a
perfect world free from all injustice to come in 1980, there
would still be those who, suffering unjustly in 1978 and
1979, would die with their wrongs unrighted. What are we
to say to them? They are not just waste products of the
creation, the shavings left on the workshop floor when the
job is done. They also have a place in the city. Their sufferings can be a participation in the victory of the Lamb. They
can be part of the witness (*marturia*) by which Christ's
victory is won. This is the great theme of the last book of the
Bible. Acts of compassion, therefore, acts by which the
church tries to share in and to bear the pain of those who
suffer, are not an escape from the real business of fighting
for liberation, or an alternative to it: they are an authentic
part of the victory of the Lamb.

It is, unfortunately, not unusual to find Christians who
condemn works of compassion because they "deflect attention from the real issue and only serve to prop up a rotten
system." There is here a lamentable mixture of naiveté in
politics and cynicism in morals. What they are really advocating is that we should exploit the misery of human
beings for political ends, on the basis of a naive belief that
the destruction of the existing structures will of itself make
way for a structure of justice. The history of the past two
hundred years does little to support this belief.

One can understand this language as a condemnation of
those who refuse to face the need for drastic changes in the
structure of society and regard the political struggle as outside of the mission of the church. This condemnation is just,
for this view implies an unbiblical and unrealistic view of
man. Real man cannot be understood apart from his place in
the public history of his time. It is totally wrong, therefore,
to separate the private from the public areas of human life
and thereby to remove politics from the sphere of Christian
responsibility. To work for the reformation of structures, to
expose and attack unjust structures, and, when the point is
reached at which all other means have failed, to work for the
overthrow of an evil political and economic order, is as

much a part of the mission of the church as to care for the sick and to feed the hungry. Part of it, but not the whole; and if the legitimate call to political action is allowed to replace the call to compassionate service, then the church has betrayed its gospel.

The goal to which we look is the city which is the perfection of all that God purposes both for our personal and for our public life. But the road from here to there is not a simple ascent. There is no evolutionary process by which the cosmos finally arrives at this goal. Our picture of history — the history that is to come — must be shaped less by the idea of evolution than by the New Testament Apocalypse. History is seen in this view under the sign of the cross. God's cause in history is not represented by the "winning side." The church is not and can never expect to be the bearer of God's cause in the sense that it is the agency through which God's order is established within history. That is the Constantinian dream. Rather, it is called to be the witness to a grace and justice which challenges, judges, and redeems the structures in which we embody our hopes for justice.

4. As I see it, the heart of the matter is exposed when we ask what happens at the Eucharist. Can the oppressor and the oppressed share together in the Eucharist? The theologians of liberation, if I understand rightly, say no. The oppressor must first cease to oppress. Like Zacchaeus he must disgorge his ill-gotten wealth. Only then can he be a communicant at the table of the Lord. I see the force of this view. If I have to question it I do so with hesitation. Yet I must do so. There are situations (and perhaps the theology of liberation comes out of such a situation) where oppression is so clear and blatant that this judgment must be made. But it is a very perilous responsibility which is taken by the man who makes this judgment. In every society, in every nation, even in every family, there is an element of oppression. We are all so made that we are conscious of the oppression of others and unconscious of the ways in which we oppress. Can there be any limit to the mutual excommuni-

cation which would follow if this principle came to be accepted? Is not the Eucharist the point at which we acknowledge the fact that we are all in sin and that we are accepted only by grace? Must this not apply even to the great matters of justice between classes, between owners and peasants? If, in effect, we identify the cause of the oppressed with the cause of God so completely that we bring forward the last judgment into today, do we not cut ourselves off from grace and pave the way for a new tyranny which acknowledges nothing higher than its own judgment?

The church lives in the midst of history as a sign, instrument, and foretaste of the reign of God. But this does not mean that in the life of the church there can be at any point in time a simple identification of the justice of God with the justice of a particular political cause. The church has too often fallen into that trap. To refuse the identification is not to fall into some kind of idealist or spiritualist illusion. It is not to detach the interior life of the soul from the business of doing justice and mercy in the life of society. It is simply to acknowledge that all human causes are ambiguous and all human actions are involved in the illusions which are the product of our egotism. It is to confess that final judgment belongs to God, and that when man usurps that prerogative he falls into a self-destructive blindness.

The issue may be put in another way. If we acknowledge the God of the Bible, we are committed to struggle for justice in society. Justice means giving to each his due. Our problem (as seen in the light of the gospel) is that each of us overestimates what is due to him as compared with what is due to his neighbor. Consequently, justice cannot be done, for everyone will judge in his own favor. Justice is done only when each one acknowledges a judge with authority over him, in relation to whose judgment he must relativize his own. It is the business of an earthly judge to represent that higher judgment. Being also a sinful human being his judgment will also be corrupted by his interest, and he may have to be overthrown in the name of the justice of God. A just society can flourish only when its members acknowledge the justice of God, which is the justice manifested and enacted in the cross. If I do not acknowledge a justice which judges the justice for which I fight, I am an agent, not of justice, but of lawless tyranny.

At this point the Christian has to be aware of the trap which is set by Marxism. I am not here questioning the Marxist analysis of the nature of capitalism, which I find very convincing; I am speaking of the Marxist understanding of man. The most obvious feature of the dedicated Marxist is his extreme moralism. For the Marxist, evil is always something external to himself. It is the "class enemy" which constitutes the locus of the evil against which he has to fight. Consequently there can be no thought of forgiveness and reconciliation. There are only two realities — the oppressor and the oppressed, the exploiter and the exploited. The oppressed and exploited are the exclusive bearers of truth and righteousness. There is no truth or righteousness *over* them, so to speak, which is able to judge and forgive them. Two things follow from this: (a) When the "oppressed" acquire power there is absolutely no check upon their use of that power. There is no righteousness over them which can judge them. The result is the kind of ruthless tyranny which we have seen under Stalin and his lesser imitators. (b) Those who identify themselves as the representatives of the "oppressed" are in a position to combine unlimited self-righteousness in respect of themselves with unlimited moral indignation in respect of their opponents. This is the most characteristic feature of the dedicated Marxist. Since there is no transcendent righteousness which can judge and forgive both the oppressor and the oppressed, the way is open for unlimited self-righteousness.

The church can only represent the righteousness of God in history in the way that Jesus did. It is enabled to do this by being constantly reincorporated into Jesus' saving action through baptism and the Eucharist and through the preaching and hearing of the Word, which explains these and applies their meaning to the actual situation. The heart of the matter is reached in the celebration of the Eucharist.

Here the ultimate horizon of grace and judgment touches the present moment. Here the church has to learn to live by the grace which forgives but does not condone sin and under the judgment which exposes sin and yet keeps open the way of repentance.

The Fifth Assembly of the World Council of Churches struggled to express its understanding of the witness of the church in face of the powers in history which deny God's justice. It said:

> The Church's unity is lived in the tension of political struggle. The Church is called to discern and attest God's purpose of justice in history and in the created world, but it is frequently tempted to remain silent in order to preserve "unity," or to divide in a crusading spirit for or against some particular cause. On these difficulties, we have three things to say:
>
> (a) Christians are sinners judged and forgiven, accepting one another as such in Christ. At the Eucharist we are all equal, a company who have no righteousness of our own but who receive by faith and in love the righteousness of God. The Church is thus the place where people with sharply opposed commitments can meet at the foot of the cross within the divine mercy which sustains them all.
>
> (b) But the Church is also a company under Christ's discipline. We are not permitted to ignore or to compromise with sin. We are called to open and vigorous mutual criticism, bearing the pain of controversy, openly testing ethical decisions (including political ones) under the truth of Christ, and seeking always the way of obedience in each concrete situation. Individual Christians may and often should take more radical positions than the Church as a whole can or should do. But there are political issues on which the Church itself must speak and act on behalf of the dignity of God's creatures. To do this is not to "politicize" the Church. Rather, the Church is politicized when it is so tied to a party or a government, a class or an ideology, that it is not free so to speak and act.
>
> (c) Open and honest controversy on political issues may lead to agreement or it may lead to polarization. When all things are brought into the light, some will find their refuge in a retreat into darkness. The Church has to learn to distinguish in the light of God's Word between sin which can be exposed and forgiven, and apostasy which rejects God's forgiveness and must therefore be rejected by the Church. How can we learn to

126

exercise this discipline and this discernment in situations where our churches are involved in racism, in social, political, or religious oppression, and in economic exploitation?[8]

The unanswered question may well close this part of my discussion; it is a warning that there is no way of arriving at a simple statement valid for all times and places about the role of the church in history. We have to learn in each situation to act and then to commit the action in faith to God our Father, in and through Jesus Christ who has taken away the sin of the world by his cross, following the leading of the Holy Spirit who alone can give us the wisdom to discern the way. The focus of this living and acting and committing will be the Eucharist. It is by faith that we confess this body, constituted by its sharing in the dying and rising of Jesus, to be the sign, instrument, and foretaste of God's reign in the midst of history. From the beginning it has been a body full of things which contradict its own nature. It is certainly no triumphant host beating down the power of evil. It shares in the character of the gospel as a whole; in it is both a disclosing and a hiddenness of God's reign. Its only sign is and must be the sign of the cross placed, not merely on its altars and its buildings, but on its corporate life.

The implication of this argument for our main theme, namely, the nature of the church's mission, is clearly this: in every situation the church must call all people — oppressor and oppressed alike — to that commitment to Jesus Christ which is expressed and sealed in baptism and continually renewed in the Eucharist. To the implications of this we will turn in the following chapter.

III

There is another aspect of liberation theology which requires examination. I have criticized its eschatology on the ground that it does not face adequately the facts of sin and

---

8. David M. Paton, ed., *Breaking Barriers: Nairobi 1975. The Official Report of the Fifth Assembly of the World Council of Churches* (Grand Rapids: Eerdmans, 1976), p. 63.

death and that its evolutionary picture of the future of man is inadequately realistic as compared with the apocalyptic view of the New Testament. We must also look critically at the other end of liberation theology — its epistemology. I have argued that one of the strong points of this theology is its insistence that theology cannot be done apart from action or, to use the favorite word, apart from "praxis." Gutierrez defines liberation theology as "critical reflection on Christian praxis in the light of the Word."[9] Its task is "to penetrate the present reality, the movement of history, that which is driving history towards the future," and this is "a new way to do theology."[10] "It is not merely," says Jose Miguez Bonino, "that theology is at the service of action. . . . Rather action is itself the truth. Truth is at the level of history, not in the realm of ideas."[11] If we ask on what the action is based or by what it is directed, Miguez answers that it is based upon a "scientific" analysis of the sociopolitical situation and for this purpose the Marxist analysis is accepted. Not that Marxism is swallowed uncritically, but "it seems to many of us that it has proved and still proves to be, the best instrument available for an effective and rational realisation of human possibilities in historical life."[12] This approach "makes possible to unmask and denounce the false theologies that cover ideologically enslaving options (theologies of the rich world, theologies of development, 'third positions' etc.)."[13] Especially emphatic is the denial of the possibility of a "third position." The *conditio sine qua non* for a true theology is to be totally committed to action for and with the oppressed on the basis of the Marxist analysis of the class struggle. Only from within this commitment can the Christian exercise a critical function in relation to Marxism. The idea that there is a "third position," committed neither to the right nor to the left, within

---

9. Gutierrez, *Theology of Liberation,* p. 13.
10. Ibid., p. 15.
11. Bonino, *Revolutionary Theology Comes of Age,* p. 72.
12. Ibid., p. 97.
13. Ibid., p. 72.

which a Christian can do theology has to be unmasked as the cover under which the interests of the oppressors lie concealed. 1. This powerfully argued position calls for much more competent examination than I am capable of, but it is not possible simply to pass it by. To begin with, it is important to recognize that this is a variant of the Marxist epistemology which already has a considerable history, even though its application to theology is only now beginning. Although Marx and Engels apparently accepted natural science as the way to knowledge of objective truth, it was inevitable that the Marxist conception of the class-conditioned character of all claims to truth should eventually affect the Marxist attitude towards science. Under Stalin the idea that natural science was an independent pathway to objective truth was denounced as bourgeois illusion. The history of science was rewritten in terms of the class struggle. The story has been told by Michael Polanyi in his book *Personal Knowledge:*

It began with scattered sniping at the more modern developments of "bourgeois science," in relativity, quantum mechanics, astronomy, psychology, and it culminated in the campaign against Mendelism. The new position was finally established when in August, 1948, Lysenko triumphantly announced to the Academy of Science that his biological views had been approved by the Central Committee of the Communist Party and members rose as one man to acclaim this decision.

The universality of science was now definitely repudiated. The claims of bourgeois science to universal validity were unmasked as deceptive ideology, while Soviet Science was directed to rely frankly on its partisan or class character. Owing to the dual mechanism of Marxism, the doctrine that all science is class science served simultaneously both to discredit bourgeois science and to accredit socialist science. Moreover, in serving the Party, science recovers — in a new sense — a claim to universality: the universality of truth is replaced by the inherently righteous and therefore historically inevitable victory of a future Communist world-government.

The dual meanings of "objectivity" and "partisanship" in this method of accrediting Soviet science are self-consistent. The

129

claims of bourgeois science to objectivity and universal validity are unmasked as false pretences on the grounds that no affirmation of science, history, or philosophy can be objective and that in reality they are always partisan weapons. At the same time, Marxism claims to have made politics into a science that bases every political action on a strictly objective assessment of the social conditions in which it has to operate, and the unmasking of bourgeois objectivity as partisan is itself an example of this Marxist objectivity. But such objectivity does not claim universality, for it would contradict itself if it claimed — for example — that the bourgeoisie could be persuaded to accept it as objective. Marxism claims for itself therefore to be objective only in the sense of being a weapon of proletarian partisanship. Neither "objectivity" nor "partisanship" is either right or wrong, it is only Socialism that is right (i.e. rising) and Capitalism that is wrong (i.e. decaying). The demand made by Stalin's régime on Soviet scholars to eschew objectivity (in the sense of universal validity) and to be guided instead by Socialist partisanship, is therefore quite consistent with the Marxist's own claims to objectivity.[14]

The disastrous consequences of this for Soviet science were recognized when the process of de-Stalinization began, and the study of the natural sciences of the USSR has now been almost completely liberated from the ideological control of Marxism. The study of the social sciences, however, remains bound, as does the pursuit of artistic interests.

2. I could wish that the theologians of liberation might reflect on the lessons of this story before insisting that theology can begin to operate only on the basis of the acceptance of the Marxist analysis. One does not need to adopt the sort of metaphysical idealism which they reject in order to deny the statement that "there is no possibility of invoking or availing oneself of a norm outside praxis itself."[15] There is the possibility (as Bonino agrees) of appealing to God's revelation of his being and his promise as witnessed in the text of Scripture. It is true, as he says, "that we

---

14. Michael Polanyi, *Personal Knowledge* (Chicago: Univ. of Chicago Press, 1958), pp. 238–239.
15. Miguez Bonino, *Revolutionary Theology Comes of Age,* p. 81.

always read a text which is already incorporated in a praxis, whether our own or someone else's," but that does not alter the fact that the text of Scripture does function and has constantly functioned as a source of judgment upon the praxis of those who have the Scriptures in their hands. Certainly the Scriptures teach — as I have insisted — that there is no knowledge of God apart from the doing of God's will. But, it seems to us, we depart from Scripture altogether if we put gospel and "scientific analysis" side by side so that the latter becomes the primary and independent source of our understanding of what is the case and what is to be done. (The matter is very much worse when, in crude popularization of liberation theology, we are told that we shall hear God speaking "in and through our human needs and aspirations."[16]) The obedience to which the gospel calls me and apart from which I cannot know God is obedience to the personal calling of Jesus Christ in and through his community. The ultimate model, in terms of which I am to understand what is the case and what is to be done, is furnished by the biblical story. This does not obviate the necessity for a scientific analysis of the political-cultural-economic reality in which I am involved, but this analysis cannot take the place of the fundamental model provided by the biblical story and cannot therefore be the ground for excluding from the communion of Christ's community those who do not accept it.

3. I am aware, of course, that the sentences I have just written are open to "unmasking" as the product of my political and economic interests as part of Western European bourgeois society. I do not deny this interest, nor my belief that in the conditions of Western Europe today (which are not those of Latin America) I am called to struggle for the development of a type of democratic society which is committed neither to Marxism nor to unrestrained capitalism. I

---

16. See the Dar-es-Salaam Statement of Third World Theologians 1976, *Study Encounter* 11, no. 3, p. 48.

acknowledge that there are situations where a Christian
may well judge that the only option for him is commitment
to the overthrow of an irreformably unjust regime. The
communion of Christians in Christ allows and requires the
mutual acknowledgment of these opposing political decisions, and I therefore reject the liberation theologians' view
that their judgment about the nature of Christian obedience
requires them to treat their opponents, not as sinners to be
corrected, but as heretics to be excluded.[17] Furthermore,
the Marxist language about "unmasking" which has been
adopted by the liberation theologians needs itself to be sub-
jected to examination. Michael Polanyi has analyzed the
remarkable way in which Marxism is able to evoke moral
passions while concealing its operations under a façade of
"scientific objectivity." The effect of this is that moral sentiments emanating from the bourgeoisie are "unmasked" as
the operation of the self-interest of a class, while the self-
interest of the proletariat is impregnated with a supreme
moral value which cannot be questioned because there is no
locus of truth outside of proletarian praxis. In relation to the
present debate, the point is important enough to justify a
lengthy quotation. To understand the process, says Polanyi,

> you must imagine that you are filled from the start — as Marx
> was — with a passion for Socialism and a horror of Capitalism.
> Looking in this light on the ideals of liberty, justice, brother-
> hood, you will observe, for example, that the Code Napoléon,
> based on these principles, was supremely effective in destroy-
> ing the feudal order and in opening the way for the bourgeoisie
> with its system of private enterprise throughout Europe. You
> will also note that it has remained the guardian of the capitalist
> order ever since. Bourgeois ideals will appear, therefore, as a
> mere superstructure of capitalism, in its opposition both to a
> feudalism whose rule it has subverted and to the proletariat,
> whose enslavement it tries to perpetuate. Bourgeois interests
> will appear to be immanent in bourgeois moral ideals. This is
> the first kind of immanence, the *negative* branch of Marxism.
>
> Think now, on the other hand, of Socialist revolutionary action.
> You are filled with a passionate desire to see the workers over-

17. Cf. Bonino, *Revolutionary Theology Comes of Age*, p. 104.

throw Capitalism and establish a realm of liberty, justice, and brotherhood. But you cannot demand this in the name of liberty, justice and brotherhood, for you despise such emotional phrases. So you must convert Socialism from a Utopia into a Science. You do so by affirming that the appropriation of the means of production by "the proletariat" will release a new flow of wealth now entrammelled by Capitalism. This affirmation satisfies the moral aspirations of Socialism, and is accepted therefore as a scientific truth by those filled with these aspirations. Moral passions are thereby cast in the form of a scientific affirmation. This is the second kind of immanence, the *positive* branch of Marxism. By covering them with a scientific disguise it protects moral sentiments against being deprecated as mere emotionalism, and gives them at the same time a sense of scientific certainty, while on the other hand it impregnates material ends with the fervour of moral passion.

One can now see that both branches of Marxism operate by denying to morality any intrinsic force of its own and that they yet both appeal in this very act to moral passions. In the first case we are presented with an analysis of bourgeois ideals in terms of immanent bourgeois interests, and because the hidden motivation of this analysis is a condemnation of capitalism, the analysis turns into an *unmasking* of bourgeois hypocrisy. Since this analysis of moral claims in terms of material interests applies quite generally, it might be thought to discredit also the moral motives of those who do the unmasking. But these motives are safe against unmasking, since they remain undeclared. Indeed, acting through the unmasking of bourgeois ideologies, they arouse powerful moral passions in others — without ever producing any moral judgment. Their propagandistic effect is achieved precisely by enunciating the unmasking in purely scientific terms, which are thus immune against suspicion of a moralizing purpose.

These supposedly scientific assertions are, of course, accepted only because they satisfy certain moral passions. We have here a *self-confirmatory reverberation* between the *theory* of bourgeois ideologies and the concealed *motives* which underlie it. This is the characteristic structure of what I shall call a dynamo-objective coupling. Alleged scientific assertions, which are accepted as such because they satisfy moral passions, will excite these passions further, and thus lend increased convincing power to the scientific affirmations in question — and so on, indefinitely. Moreover, such a dynamo-objective coupling is also potent in its own defence. Any criticism of its scientific part is rebutted by the moral passions behind it, while any moral objections are coldly brushed aside by invoking the inexorable verdict of its scientific findings. Each of the two components, the dynamic and the objective, takes it in turn to draw attention away from the other when it is under attack.[18]

In accepting as a starting point for their theology the Marxist analysis of the sociopolitical situation, liberation theologians have armed themselves with a weapon against which the bourgeois theologian may easily find himself helpless. He can, of course, point to what happens when Marxist ideas are clothed with political power. But this is not as easy as it seems, for other Marxist states have probably learned from the experience of the USSR that "de-Stalinization" or its equivalent is too dangerous to be allowed. The new rulers of China seem to be solving the problem by using the "Gang of Four" as scapegoats for policies which everyone knows were those of Mao Tse-tung. Marxist practice has its own ways of discrediting such bourgeois concepts as "human rights" and "free enquiry." In spite of this vulnerability I must insist that the Marxist epistemology, which has been thoroughly discredited in respect of the natural sciences, cannot now be consecrated as the new way of "doing theology." It is not in dispute that true theology can only be done in the context of praxis. There can be no "academic theology," if that means theology divorced from commitment, faith, and obedience. On this issue the liberation theologians are right. Where I think they are wrong is in the identification of this commitment with acceptance of the Marxist analysis of society. The commitment is not to a cause or to a program: it is to a person. At the heart of mission there must always be the call to be committed to Jesus Christ in his community. It is at this aspect of the matter that we must now look.

---

18. Polanyi, *Personal Knowledge*, pp. 229-230.

9

Church Growth, Conversion and Culture

MISSION IS the proclaiming of the kingdom of the Father, and it concerns the rule of God over all that is. We have seen, therefore, that the church has been led by the logic of its own gospel to move beyond preaching into actions of all kinds for the doing of God's justice in the life of the world.

But mission is also sharing the life of the Son, for it is in Jesus that God's kingdom is present in the life of the world and this presence is continued — under the sign of the cross — in the community which confesses Jesus as Lord and belongs to him as his body. We have therefore to speak about this community, how it grows and is sustained in its mission. It is futile to talk about the task of the church as agent of liberation — in whatever terms we understand that task — unless we also pay attention to the ways in which the church in any place comes into being and grows. It is useless to talk about the task if you are not concerned about the agency which is to carry out the task. We have to ask not only "What is to be done?" but also "Who is to do it?" The opening announcement of the gospel, "the kingdom of God is at hand," is followed at once by a call addressed personally to Peter and Andrew, James and John to follow Jesus

135

and to share in the work of the kingdom. The calling of men and women to be converted, to follow Jesus, and to be part of his community is and must always be at the center of mission.

One of today's most influential schools of missiology takes this as its central emphasis. The Institute of Church Growth of the School of World Missions, located at Fuller Theological Seminary and under the leadership of Dr. Donald McGavran, has forced missionary agencies in many parts of the world to ask why churches do not grow and to plan deliberately for church growth and expect it as the normal experience of missions. Dr. McGavran's convictions were developed out of his experience in India, where he observed that some churches were multiplying rapidly while others in similar situations stagnated. He saw that these contrasting experiences resulted from contrasting missionary methods. On the one hand there was the method which was centered in the "mission station." (Since "mission" means going and "station" means standing still, one might think that "mission station" was the perfect contradiction in terms. It has been, nevertheless, the central element in the program of missions during most of the modern period.) In the "mission station" approach, as McGavran sees it, converts are detached from the natural communities to which they belong, attached to the foreign mission and its institutions, and required to conform to ethical and cultural standards which belong to the Christianity of the foreign missionary. The effect of this policy is twofold. On the one hand the convert, having been transplanted into an alien culture, is no longer in a position to influence his non-Christian relatives and neighbors; on the other hand the energies of the mission are exhausted in the effort to bring the converts, or more often their children, into conformity with the standards supposed by the missionaries to be required by the gospel. Both factors have the effect of stopping the growth of the church. Schools, colleges, hospitals, and programs for social action multiply, but the church does not. McGavran traces this failure to a misreading of the Great Commission. According to the text of Matthew 28:18–20, Jesus instructed his apostles to disciple the nations, to baptize, and to teach. The order of these three words represents an order of priorities which must be observed. The primary business of missions is to disciple and baptize. Teaching must follow, not precede the others. It is no doubt the task of the church to teach men to observe all that Jesus has commanded, but this can come only after they have been made part of the church. The "mission station" strategy has resulted in the stopping of growth because missions have devoted themselves to perfecting the energies which should have been given to discipling. By contrast, the strategy of the "people's movement" actively seeks and fosters the corporate decisions of whole social groups to accept the gospel. This avoids the breaking of natural relationships. "Men become Christians without social dislocation so that the resulting churches have leaders and loyalties intact. Churches are therefore likely to be more stable and self-supporting and to bear up better under persecution."[1] Churches which are the products of such people's movements tend to grow, and in fact the great majority of those who have become Christians from among the non-Christian religions have come in this way.

In a paper prepared for the International Congress on World Evangelization (Lausanne, 1974) McGavran spelled out his essential concern in the following theses:

(a) Huge numbers of people remain in ignorance of the gospel and they will not be reached by their Christian neighbors.

(b) They must hear the gospel in terms of their own cultures, for "God accepts world cultures."

(c) Therefore there must be deliberate crossing of cultural frontiers: the natural growth of churches through contacts within the same culture will not accomplish this.

---

1. Donald McGavran, in *Concise Dictionary of the Christian World Mission*, ed. S. Neill et al. (London: Lutterworth Press, 1971), p. 479.

(d) The aim must be that in every piece of the cultural mosaic which makes up human existence there shall be "Christian Churches which fit that piece and are closely adapted to its culture."

(e) The future belongs to the masses. They have "a built-in receptivity to the Good News." Therefore enormous growth is possible if the right methods are followed.

To this brief summary of McGavran's thought, which has been developed in many volumes relating to different situations, it should be added that he has consistently urged that the resources available for mission should be applied in places where rapid church growth is possible and to methods which will favor its occurrence. The specific task of missions is to "disciple the nations." Their work must be judged by their success in doing just that.

If I have given anything like a fair summary of the teaching of the Church Growth school of missiology. I hope I have shown that it contains important elements of truth. The criticism of the "mission station" strategy has a great deal of force. It is also true that missions have, in McGavran's phrase, tended to put perfecting before discipling and thereby fallen into the old legalist trap. They have become the proponents of a new law rather than of a liberating gospel. The church has been made to appear more like a school where examinations have to be passed than like a place where the community meets to celebrate its freedom.

Moreover, it is right that Christians should continually be asked why their churches do not grow and why they are so little concerned about the multitudes who have not heard the gospel or who, having heard it, have rejected it.

The Church Growth school of missiology raised basic questions in at least three fields:

I The relation of numerical church growth to the message of the kingdom.
II The meaning of conversion, and the relation between discipling and perfecting.

III The relation of gospel and church to culture. We shall look at these three issues in turn.

I

1. There can surely be no doubt that anyone who is committed to a cause will rejoice when the number of those so committed multiplies. And anyone who knows Jesus as Lord and Savior will rejoice when men come to know him and will grieve when he is ignored or rejected. This is something which surely cannot be gainsaid. And when we turn to the story of the first days of the church as we have it in the Acts of the Apostles, we find a lively interest in numerical growth. On the day of Pentecost, we are told, three thousand people were added to the church (2:41), and as days went by "the Lord added to their number day by day those who were being saved" (2:47). Shortly afterwards we learn that the believing men numbered five thousand (4:4), and again we are told that "the disciples were increasing in number" (6:1) and that "the number of the disciples multiplied greatly" (6:7). After the arrest and release of Peter we are again told that "the word of God grew and multiplied" (12:24), and at the beginning of Paul's second missionary journey it is said that the churches in Syria and Cilicia "increased in numbers daily" (6:5).

But when one has given due weight to this obvious delight in the numerical growth of the church, one must also observe that the rest of the New Testament furnishes little evidence of interest in numerical growth. In the Synoptic Gospels Jesus does not give the impression of being interested in large numbers. There is implied delight in the marvelous multiplication of the seed that falls into good ground (Mark 4:8) but also explicit joy over one single sheep that was lost and is found (Luke 15:3-7). It is indeed interesting that Luke, who shows such evident delight in recording the multiplication of believers after Pentecost, also records several sayings of Jesus which suggest that the

139

coming of God's kingdom does not at all depend on the number of those who expect it and pray for it. "Fear not, little flock, for it is your Father's good pleasure to give you the kingdom" (Luke 12:32). "When the Son of Man comes, will he find faith on the earth?" (Luke 18:8). The emphasis falls upon the faithfulness of the disciples rather than upon their numbers.

Neither does a study of the Epistles seem to disclose any interest in numerical growth. We do not find Paul concerning himself with the size of the churches, or with questions about their growth. His primary concern is with their faithfulness, with the integrity of their witness. His own concern is that he may "fully [preach] the gospel of Christ" so that "the offering of the Gentiles may be acceptable, sanctified by the Holy Spirit" (Rom. 15:15–19). He is willing to "become all things to all men" that he may "by all means save some" (I Cor. 9:22), but all of this is "for the sake of the gospel, that I may share in its blessings" (9:23). In the first letter of Peter the believers are told always to "be prepared to make a defense to any one who calls you to account for the hope that is in you . . . with gentleness and reverence" (I Pet. 3:15). There is a deep concern for the integrity of the Christian witness, but there is no evidence of anxiety about or enthusiasm for rapid numerical growth. In no sense does the triumph of God's reign seem to depend upon the growth of the church.

In the Johannine Gospel and letters there is a persistent concern about the world, for which and into which the Father has sent the Son and the Son has sent the church. But there is nowhere any suggestion that the salvation of the world depends upon the growth of the church.

Reviewing, then, the teaching of the New Testament, one would have to say that, on the one hand, there is joy in the rapid growth of the church in its earliest days, but that, on the other, there is no evidence that the numerical growth of the church is a matter of primary concern. There is no shred of evidence in Paul's letters to suggest that he judged the churches by the measure of their success in rapid numerical growth, nor is there anything comparable to the strident cries of some contemporary evangelists that the salvation of the world depends upon the multiplication of believers. There is an incomparable sense of seriousness and urgency as the apostle contemplates the fact that he and all men "must appear before the judgment seat of Christ" and as he acknowledges the constraint of Jesus' love and the ministry of reconciliation which he has received (II Cor. 5:10–21). But this nowhere appears as either an anxiety or an enthusiasm about the numerical growth of the church.

2. If we turn from the New Testament to the later pages of church history, we find, of course, periods of rapid numerical growth, of no growth, and of diminishing numbers. In the period following the conversion of Constantine the churches multiplied. So did they at certain times during the conversion of the tribes of northwest Europe, and during the Spanish conquest of Central and South America. We do not look back on these periods with great satisfaction. It might be argued that, for example, the peoples of Central and South America who were baptized by the thousands in the time of the *conquistadores* were not truly converted. But this fails to take account of McGavran's argument that discipling must precede "perfecting." On McGavran's principles it is difficult to see how one could fault the procedure of the Spanish and Portuguese missionaries. And it is a matter of historical fact that many groups which were originally Christianized in this way have become and remained strong and vital Christian communities. The fisher-folk of the Coramandel Coast — the Paravas — were baptized en masse in 1534 as a condition of Portuguese protection from Muslim raiders. The task of teaching them the elements of the faith was taken up only eight years later by Francis Xavier, but they have remained among the strongest and most stable Christian communities in India. McGavran's argument has certainly much to commend it, and yet it is surely also true that the church is least recognizable as the body of Christ when it is growing rapidly through the influence of military, political, and economic power.

And, even apart from such examples of rapid growth through mainly secular influences, we have to ask whether the church is most faithful in its witness to the crucified and risen Jesus and most recognizable as the community which "bears about in the body the dying of Jesus" when it is chiefly concerned with its own self-aggrandizement. When numerical growth is taken as the criterion of judgment on the church, we are transported with alarming ease into the world of the military campaign or the commercial sales drive. Sentences such as the following may be acceptable in the board room of a powerful mission agency with plenty of resources, but they sound quite different to those who are at the receiving end of the operation: "Unresponsive areas should be *occupied lightly*. A *blitzkrieg* of missionaries in a resistant area usually serves to alarm the religious leaders and to harden the people in their unbelief. Better to keep the witness there *light*, ready to move in heavy reinforcements when the culture turns responsive."[2]

3. I come back to the very simple point which I made at the beginning of this discussion. Anyone who knows Jesus Christ as his Lord and Savior must desire ardently that others should share that knowledge and must rejoice when the number of those who do is multiplied. Where this desire and this rejoicing are absent, we must ask whether something is not wrong at the very center of the church's life. McGavran is therefore right to press upon us the question, Why is there not more concern for the multiplication of believers and more evidence of its happening? He is right also in his criticism of missions for adopting practices which put in the center, not a liberating gospel, but a series of demands for conformity to ethical and cultural standards set by the missionary. He is right in insisting that the missionary has a specific task — not the whole task of evangelism, nurture, prophetic witness, and action for justice and compassion, but the more limited task of "discipling." This is not to deny

---

2. M. R. Bradshaw, *Church Growth through Evangelism in Depth* (S. Pasadena: William Carey Library, 1969), p. 30.

that the others named and many more must be included in any full statement of the church's calling; it is only to insist that within the broader spectrum of the church's calling the missionary has a specific and more limited calling. He is to "disciple the nations." The other things must not be left undone, but they must not deflect the missionary from the essential thing to which he is called — to bring "the nations" into allegiance to Jesus Christ.

There is a partial — but not, I think, a total — correspondence between this and the survey which Paul makes of his own missionary work. In writing to the church at Rome about his travel plans, Paul says that he has "fully preached the gospel of Christ" all the way from Jerusalem to Illyricum, and that therefore he has "no longer any room for work in these regions" (Rom. 15:17–23). Paul can say that he has finished his work as a missionary in a specific region. Clearly he does *not* mean any of the following three things: that all the inhabitants of the region have been converted, baptized, and incorporated in the church; that all those who have been baptized are now fully mature Christians for whom no more "perfecting" is needed; that everyone in the region has heard the gospel. In what sense, then, can he be said to have finished his work? In the light of all we can know about the preaching and practice of Paul, we would have to answer by saying that through his preaching and through the work of the Holy Spirit there have been formed throughout the region communities of men and women who are being offered acceptably to God as the firstfruit of the Gentiles. It is the coming to birth of these communities of the saints — those whom God has called and claimed as his own — which is the fruit of his work. Others may come after him and build on the foundation he has laid, as Apollos did in Corinth (I Cor. 3:5–15). His task as a missionary is clear, limited, and — literally — fundamental. He is sent to lay the foundation stone of the church, and that stone is Christ. The result of his work, in other words, will be a community which acknowledges Jesus Christ as the supreme Lord of life. When this community exists, the missionary has done the work for which he was sent.

4. This discussion of Paul's understanding of his apostolic calling prompts a reference to another missiologist who like McGavran was a persistent critic of the missionary methods of the nineteenth and early twentieth centuries. Roland Allen (1868–1947) served as a missionary in China until 1903. Thereafter he did not (like McGavran) found an institute, but he wrote a succession of books and articles arguing with great persistence that the methods of contemporary mission were not those of Paul. He contrasted what Paul achieved in ten years of work with what modern missions had failed to achieve in a century. Paul could say that in four great provinces he had completed his work. By contrast, missions in Asia were still only at the beginning and no end was in sight. What was the reason for the difference?

As Allen looked at Paul's missionary methods he saw four decisive points of difference from modern methods.

(a) When, as the result of the preaching of the gospel, a Christian community has come into being, Paul entrusts the whole responsibility to the local leadership and moves on. He does not do what modern missionaries have done; he does not build a bungalow! The new converts are simply "committed to the Lord in whom they believed" (Acts 14:23), and the missionary moves on. His work is done.

(b) Paul does not establish financial relations with the new church. There are no subsidies or grants-in-aid. By becoming Christians the new converts do not lose their independence.

(c) Nor do they lose their status as adults. They are not treated as children. At no point does Paul lay down laws in the manner of the ten commandments. When he is consulted he advises, but his advice is largely based on the ethical teaching generally acknowledged in surrounding society. Even on the question of contact with idolatry he does not lay down authoritative rules but appeals to their own best judgment (I Cor. 10:14–22). In spite of the decrees of

Acts 15:29, Paul refrains from legislating in any binding manner on the subject of food offered to idols (I Cor. 8). Even when, as in his dealings with the Galatians, he has to charge them with what could amount to apostasy, his language shows that he sees them as adults who must be reasoned with, not as subordinates who can be commanded. The fact that he speaks of them as children with whom he is again in travail is vivid testimony to his own spiritual anguish, but the argument which immediately follows is addressed to mature men and women capable of following a subtle and passionate argument (Gal. 3 and 4). All of this is very far from the style in which missionaries have often claimed to direct the development of "their" converts.

(d) Finally — and perhaps most important — Paul does not impose on them a ministry chosen and trained by himself. He has his colleagues and helpers — Timothy, Titus, Tychicus, and the rest — but they are available to be sent from church to church on special missions. The local ministry of each church is formed from its own membership. In contrast to this, modern missions have insisted on the necessity for training a new kind of leadership in schools and seminaries directed by the foreign missionary on the basis of his perception of ethical and intellectual priorities. Consequently, whereas the churches formed by the work of modern missions have been able to develop a fully native ministerial leadership only after decades and even centuries of training, Paul could address the church in Philippi "with the bishops and deacons" within a very few years of the first conversions.

The central thrust of all Roland Allen's writing is expressed in the title of a posthumously published work, *The Ministry of the Spirit.* Allen's charge against modern missions was that they had been tempted by their alliance with colonial powers to act as though the mission of the church could be pursued in the style of a cultural and educational campaign, as though the object was to multiply replicas of the sending churches. In contrast to this Allen rightly saw that in the New Testament portrayal of mission the central

145

reality is the active work of the living Holy Spirit himself. It is the Spirit who brings about conversion, the Spirit who equips those who are called with the gifts needed for all the varied forms of ministry, and the Spirit who guides the church into all the truth. The Spirit is not the property of the sending church or of the missionary who is sent. It is not part of the missionary's duty to mold the new church into the style of the old. The Spirit is sovereign and free, and the missionary must trust the Spirit to do his own work. Where Christ is confessed, where the word of the gospel is preached and the sacraments of the gospel are administered, and where there is a ministry which links the new community to the wider fellowship of the catholic church, there, Allen believed, the Holy Spirit must be trusted to provide all that is needed, and the missionary has done his work and can move on.

Allen was not much heeded in the days when missions could still count on the superior power and wealth of the colonizing nations. Those who have served as missionaries through the years of decolonization have been better placed to listen to his words. In my own experience of evangelism in South Indian villages I have seen how the gospel can spread and living churches can be multiplied and grow if one is willing to refrain from imposing Western patterns of ministry and training, and to allow those whom the Spirit touches within the life of village communities to develop styles of leadership congruous with the native culture. I have seen enough to be convinced that Roland Allen's central thesis is true.

(5) It is clear that there are important differences between Allen and McGavran. Allen is not primarily concerned about numerical growth; he is concerned about the conditions under which spontaneously growing churches come to be born and to develop. But what they have in common is the conviction that missions have been wrong in their insistence that it is their business to impose on younger churches ethical standards laid down by the sending churches as an essential part of their work. In the language of McGavran, they have confused "discipling" with

"perfecting." In Allen's language, they have relied on the pressure of the law to mold new churches into conformity to Christ, when they should have trusted the power of the Holy Spirit working through the Word and sacraments of the gospel in the life of the community. Both of them therefore stand together in the sharpest possible antithesis to the theologians of liberation, for whom the essential commitment is to action for God's justice in the life of the world. The true church consists of those who are so committed. Only this is "to know the Lord." Those who claim to be Christians in virtue of baptism and church membership but arc not so committed arc no part of the true church. They may cry "Lord, Lord," but they do not do the Father's will and in spite of all their piety the Lord whom they claim to know disowns them (Matt. 7:21–23). For both Allen and McGavran, on the other hand, the essential commitment is to Jesus Christ in the fellowship of his people. Right action for the doing of God's will in the life of the world will follow from this. McGavran would agree that Christians must be involved in the struggle to build a just society but insists that "the most potent element in that struggle, namely multitudes of Christian cells where men meet around the Bible to seek the will of God and to open themselves to his righteousness and power," must not be denied to them.[3] In spite of mutual acknowledgment of the truth in each other's views, McGavran and Allen lead out into sharply diverging lines of action and to deep mutual distrust and antagonism. The matter in question is the ethical context and content of conversion, and to this we must now turn.

II

1. In her book *Theology in an Industrial Society* Margaret Kane outlines two contrasting ways of understanding the church's mission. The two are summarized in parallel columns as follows:

---

3. Lausanne Congress, paper on "The Dimensions of World Evangelization."

A	B
Revelation	
God is known through unchanging propositions, handed on from the past in large abstract concepts—sin, judgment, repentance, redemption, etc.	God is known by personal meeting in and through persons and events in the present
Theology	
is a study of the Bible and what people have made of it	is a continuing process of interpreting contemporary experiences in the light of God's revelation in Christ...
is to be done by academic experts	is to be done by everyone
The Church	
consists of those called out of an evil world	sharp distinctions between those who do or do not belong to the church are not helpful
its task is to obey the command to preach the gospel	the church's job is to penetrate the world and point to the signs of God's activity in it
to save souls out of the world	the whole creation is to be redeemed
to do this it must build up its own organization in a disciplined way	
clergy are leaders and laymen must help them	laymen have a crucial ministry in the world and clergy must help them
Man	
the soul is the important part of man and he must beware of the body and materialism	man is a total person, body and spirit
man is an isolated individual	man's life only has meaning in relation to his total social and historical context
Jesus Christ	
divinity is stressed	humanity is stressed[4]

---

4. Margaret Kane, *Theology in an Industrial Society* (London: SCM Press, 1975), pp. 31-32.

While not giving an unconditional endorsement of *B*, Miss Kane insists that although *A* is the typical attitude of church people, the points made in *B* are essential for any relevant style of mission in contemporary society. A similar concern is expressed by many in the demand for a "contextual theology," by which is meant a theology which gives primary attention to the issues which people are facing at that time and place and insists that the gospel cannot be communicated except in terms of these issues. In the correspondence between M. M. Thomas and Hendrikus Berkhof which followed the Mexico conference of 1963, the former repeatedly insisted that we have to begin by asking "What is the form and content of the salvation which Christ offers to men in the secular world?" and that we can only answer that question by looking at the actual needs and aspirations of this man. In fact, these aspirations are in one sense or another the creation of the gospel, and "the Message comes alive at the cutting edge between the Gospel and the quest of modern man for a truly human existence." Indeed, "nobody *knows* the Message in a historical vacuum."[5] It is on the basis of such convictions as these that the advocates of "contextual theology" are suspicious of traditional forms of evangelism which appear to consist of the repetition of "unchanging propositions handed down from the past" and to evade the obligation to "penetrate the world and point to the signs of God's activity in it." For this kind of evangelism, it is held, is irrelevant to the actual decisions which men and women must make if they are to act in line with what God is doing in the world now and to the actual form which "salvation" must take if it is to appear as salvation for contemporary human beings. It is obvious that from this point of view McGavran's separation of "discipling" from "perfecting" and Allen's insistence that the duty of the missionary is finished when a living church has come into being are both to be condemned. Both of these,

---

5. M. M. Thomas in *Secular Man and Christian Mission*, ed. Paul Loeffler (New York: Friendship Press, 1968), pp. 19, 22–23.

in this view, could be quite irrelevant to the real business of mission, which is concerned with men's response through decision and action to what God is doing in the life of the secular world now.

I feel the force of this argument very acutely. Any critic of traditional styles of evangelism can easily point to examples of conversion which are not merely irrelevant but actually counterproductive in relation to the real ethical issues of the time and place. It is notorious that the times and places from which successful evangelistic campaigns and mass conversions have been reported have often been marked by flagrant evils such as racism, militant sectarianism, and blind support of oppressive economic and political systems. How are we to evaluate a form of evangelism which produces baptized, communicant, Bible-reading, and zealous Christians who are committed to church growth but uncommitted to radical obedience to the plain teaching of the Bible on the issues of human dignity and social justice? And how can we defend a form of evangelism which has nothing to say about the big issues of public righteousness and talks only of questions of personal and domestic behavior? Can we agree that the big ethical issues are secondary matters which can be attended to after conversion? Can there be any real "discipling" which does not include as an essential element the ethical commitments which McGavran puts into the category of "perfecting?" Is there — and here we must listen again to the Latin Americans — is there any knowledge of God which is not *at the same time* the doing of God's will? Can "discipling" and "perfecting" be separated even for a moment? Can there be any preaching of the "text" of the gospel except in an explicit relation to the "context" of the contemporary world?

These questions imply their answers. There cannot be a separation between conversion and obedience. To be converted in any sense which is true to the Bible is something which involves the whole person. It is a total change of direction which includes both the inner reorientation of the

150

heart and mind and the outward reorientation of conduct in all areas of life. The original announcement of the gospel ("the reign of God is at hand") led immediately to a call to be converted ("repent"), to believe in the present reality of God's reign, and to follow Jesus. All of these belong together as part of one single action. The call to conversion is not given in a vacuum. It is in the context of a call to follow Jesus, and what is meant by following Jesus is spelled out in his teaching and example.

2. What are the implications of this? Does it mean that conversion *is* essentially a matter of ethical choice, a decision to act in a different way? It certainly means following Jesus, but what concretely does this mean for a man or woman in an African village or a South American *favella* now? There have always been missionaries and evangelists who were sure they knew the answer. The answers have covered an almost infinite spectrum of ethical issues from drink, gambling, and dancing through polygamy and circumcision to commitment to the battle against communism, racism, or fascism. The answers varied widely but the accent was always firm: "until you have abandoned A, B, and C and accepted X, Y, and Z, you cannot be regarded as a truly converted Christian." Looked at from another time or place this is easily recognized as the old substitution of law for gospel against which Paul had to fight in the first days of the church. From a distance one can easily see the relative character of the ethical choices and one can condemn the evangelists who falsely absolutized them. One can also see how time and again the law brings death and not life when it is put in the place of the gospel. The church becomes the agent of a moral crusade which divides mankind into allies and enemies instead of being a body of people who can be agents of liberation for all without distinction because they are themselves liberated from bondage to law. It is easy to see this from a distance. It is much harder to see how the church here and now can escape from this kind of legalism without becoming ethically irresponsible. Can there be any true conversion which does not involve, *here and now*, a new

way of behaving and therefore a new decision on the ethical and political issues of this time and place?

No, there cannot. There are not two stages in conversion, one religious and the second ethical. To that question there can be only one answer. But a new question has now to be put: Who has the right to decide the ethical content of conversion at any time or place — the evangelist or the convert? The place where the virus of legalism gets into the work of evangelism is the place where the evangelist presumes that he has that right, that he knows in advance and can tell the potential convert what the ethical content of conversion will be. This is what has happened over and over again. The missionary has had the power and has believed that he had the right to lay down the ethical preconditions for baptism. He has thought that he was lord over the gospel instead of being its servant. He has failed to realize that the living Christ, speaking through the Scriptures, can speak directly to the new convert in a way which is not just an echo of the words of the missionary. At this point we have to listen to the witness of converts as much as to that of evangelists. If we do so we shall find that in many instances the impact of the life and teaching of Jesus has led the convert to understand the ethical content of conversion in a way markedly different from the way it was presented by the missionary.

In his account of the beginnings of Christianity in Uganda, John V. Taylor has shown very vividly how the first converts (most of whom were young men at the court of the Kabaka) felt the demand of the gospel upon their consciences in ways which had little connection with the ethical teaching of the missionaries. The latter laid great stress on the necessity for an immediate abandonment of polygamy as the condition for baptism. But in the hearts and consciences of the converts other questions were being raised by the gospel and especially by the teaching and example of Jesus himself. They saw in him a new pattern of behavior calling for humility and for willingness to share the work and the hardship of the poor. They saw that slavery was incompatible with allegiance to Christ, and they found themselves engaged in a deep inner struggle between the "old man" and the "new man in Christ" of which the missionary was only dimly aware.[6]

Who has the right to decide the ethical content of conscience? Most modern missions have assumed that the church which is entrusted with the gospel has this right. McGavran and Allen deny this, and I think they have the New Testament on their side. I must refer here to what was said in Chapter 6 about the work of the Holy Spirit in mission and particularly about the story of Peter and Cornelius. If the church which is the bearer of the gospel has also the right to lay down for new converts the ethical implications of conversion, the mission has become simply church extension. I have insisted that to regard it so is to fail to acknowledge the sovereign freedom of the Holy Spirit, who in his own way brings the truth and power of the gospel home to the hearts and minds of people outside the church and gives them fresh insights into the will of God by which the church itself is corrected and its understanding of the gospel is enlarged. If this is denied we become victims of the very human and understandable but fatal error against which Paul had to fight on behalf of the Gentile converts for their freedom in the gospel. Paul insisted in this struggle that he was maintaining the absolute supremacy and finality of Christ. The preaching of the gospel of Christ cannot be made auxiliary to the fulfillment of the law. Christ is seen to be the fulfiller of the law only when he has been seen to be the end of the law.

Most missiology has been written by missionaries rather than by converts. If we had attended more dilligently to the testimony of the latter we would have learned that the experience of conversion to Christ does indeed have a necessary ethical content. It does mean a new way of acting. But the point of ethical crisis is often quite different from

---

6. John V. Taylor, *The Growth of the Church in Buganda* (London: SCM Press, 1958), pp. 45–49.

the one in the mind of the missionary. This is especially true in cases where the work of the missionary includes the delivery of the written Scriptures. In these cases the missionary may find that the point at which the conscience of the convert has been awakened is far away from the point which seemed to him to be crucial.

3. I am pleading for a recognition of the sovereignty and freedom of the Holy Spirit to bring the word of God in Jesus Christ to the consciences of men in his own way. I am insisting that the work of evangelism must never become a crusade to persuade people to adopt the ethical stances of the evangelist. I am drawing attention to those times and places where the church, in a pathetic pursuit of "relevance," has tried to gain a hearing for the gospel by latching it on to some contemporary political enthusiasm. And I am recalling also those times and places at which the church has so identified the gospel with a particular ethical or political program that it has been filled more with hard and censorious fanaticism than with the joyful assurance of abounding grace to sinful men and women.

And yet I know that there is a danger of deceiving myself when I speak about the freedom and sovereignty of the gospel. The gospel is preached by men and women whose corporate life reflects certain ethical priorities. They may be honestly convinced that they are simply preaching Christ, but the Christ whom they preach will be seen to reflect the kind of values they cherish. Even in preaching Christ they will be, knowingly or unknowingly, advocating their own beliefs about what is good and true and desirable. And if their beliefs are such that they fail to take account of the real powers at work in society, their preaching of Christ will be — to that extent — irrelevant to the real ethical choices to which God is calling men.

And yet again, our limited and distorted images of Christ do not destroy his sovereign freedom and power. Paul can rejoice when Christ is preached even insincerely, for Christ is greater than our understanding of him. This is a matter both for encouragement and for warning: encouragement because the sins which deface the church do not destroy the power of the gospel; warning that the church must be ready and expect to receive correction from the converts. Even when the church has done its best to discern the signs of the times, to understand what are the powers at work in the world, and to point to the issues where decisions have to be made in the conflict between the reign of God and the power of evil, this understanding is partial, limited, and distorted. The human situation is more complex and subtle than even the best Christian analysis can penetrate. Therefore the church cannot make a total identification of conversion to Christ with a particular set of ethical decisions based on its own analysis. It must speak to the best of its ability about what obedience to Christ will involve. But it must also recognize that its own ethical perceptions are limited and blurred by its own sinful self-interest. In preaching Christ it will certainly make clear (perhaps more effectively by example than by word) that conversion will have ethical implications. But it must also be ready to be surprised by the fresh insights of the converts into the ethical implications of the gospel and must expect to have to revise and correct its own patterns of obedience. This point is obscured when we think of mission in terms of "foreign missions." In this case the sending church is insulated from the correction which it needs to receive from the new converts. Mission, as I have insisted, is not just church extension. It is an action in which the Holy Spirit does new things, brings into being new kinds of obedience. But the new gifts are for the whole body and not just for the new members. Mission involves learning as well as teaching, receiving as well as giving.

4. The church misunderstands itself if it thinks that it is itself the place where the truth and righteousness of the reign of God is embodied as against the reign of evil in the world. This ancient temptation to identify the church with the kingdom of God seems to be present again in some manifestations of the theology of liberation. The relation of the church to the kingdom is a more complex one and, I am

convinced, can be truly grasped only by means of the trinitarian model.

Conversion is to Christ. It is primarily and essentially a personal event in which a human person is laid hold of by the living Lord Jesus Christ at the very center of his being and turned towards him in loving trust and obedience. Christ is the Son of the Father by whom all things are made, sustained, and ordered towards their true end, anointed by the Spirit to proclaim the kingdom of his Father and to manifest it in bearing upon himself the sin of the world.

Conversion to Christ is therefore also commitment to be with him and with all who are so committed in continuing in the power of the same anointing, proclaiming, and bearing. It is commitment to follow Jesus, with all who are so committed, along the way of the cross — the way of fearless and trustful encountering and enduring the power of evil in the contemporary world.

The company of those so committed and so following does not possess in itself the fullness of understanding or of obedience. It is a learning community. Part of that learning will be the prophetic discernment in the power of the Spirit of the issues where evil is to be encountered and endured. Part of it will be the receiving of correction and enlargement by those whom the Spirit calls into discipleship. The Spirit is not the property of the community but is its lord and guide, going ahead of the church and using both its proclamation and its endurance to bring fresh people to conversion. The church cannot lay down in advance for such people what commitment will mean but must, like Peter in the house of Cornelius, learn from them new lessons about its own obedience. As a learning community which can only press forward from partial to fuller understanding of the Father's reign, the church will know that it cannot impose its own ethical insights at any one time and place upon those whom the Spirit calls into its company. It must always press on towards fuller obedience but at the same time proclaim Christ as Lord above and beyond its own faulty obedience, and expect and welcome the correction of them whom the Spirit calls into commitment to Christ.

I am bound to conclude, therefore, that Roland Allen is right in saying that a missionary's work is done when there has been called into being in any place a living church furnished with the means (Scripture, sacraments, and a ministry linking it with the universal church) by which it may learn and grow in obedience to Christ. I cannot find, on the other hand, that McGavran is right in his insistence upon numerical growth as the criterion of success in mission or in the way "discipling" and "perfecting" are related in his writings. For the essential witness of the church which the Holy Spirit takes and uses to bring men to conversion is the witness (*marturia*) given when proclamation is linked to the full ministry of the suffering Servant of the Lord who discerns, encounters, and bears in his body the sin by which the world rejects God's rule. The church's struggle towards "perfecting" in the sense of being more perfectly conformed to the model of the suffering Servant of the Lord can never be in competition with the work of "discipling," which is in fact not our work but that of the Holy Spirit himself.

III

We come now to the third issue raised by the Church Growth school of missiologists, namely, that of the relation between conversion and culture. No one can deny the truth of McGavran's thesis that the growth of the church has often been grievously hindered because of a failure to recognize and honor differences of culture. The consequence of this failure is that conversion separates the convert from his own culture, robs him of a great part of his human inheritance, and makes him a second-class adherent of an alien culture.

Like many earlier missiologists McGavran draws attention to the fact that the Great Commission includes the command to "disciple the nations." The implication is that those who are to become disciples are not individuals considered in isolation, but human beings whose nationhood is part of their being. The gospel, therefore, is to be addressed to the whole human community, since the real human life of its people is bound up inextricably with the language and culture of the whole. There is a strong tradition in German missiology which has laid great emphasis on this. Gustav Warneck (1834–1910), generally regarded as the founder of Protestant missiology, insisted that the ties which hold society together should as far as possible be preserved and that the aim should be the conversion and baptism of whole communities rather than of individuals. The great work of Christian Keysser (1877–1961) in the highlands of New Guinea was based on the principle of "tribal conversion," according to which the whole community is brought to the point of accepting Christianity and only after this are individual members baptized. In this way everything possible is done to avoid the disruption of the culture and social organization of the people. Perhaps the extreme example of this method is the work of Bruno Gutmann (1876–1966) among the Chagga people of Tanzania. Gutmann believed that the basic forms of tribe, neighborhood, and age group were part of the God-given order of creation, and that the work of missions is to build upon and to perfect these created realities. From this point of view such ideas as "civilization" and "development" represent the enemy against which missions must guard the peoples among whom they work.

It is beyond question that missions conducted on these principles have led to the formation of strong, stable, and growing churches. But the dangers are obvious. Gutmann's basic created forms are easily recognizable as Hitler's "blood and soil," and theologians like Karl Barth have denounced such doctrines. To ascribe absolute value to the forms of social organization at any one time and place is both historically naive and theologically intolerable. All social organization is subject to change, and it is absurd to describe a particular manifestation as part of an unalterable order of creation.

More seriously, this is intolerable from a theological point of view; it is to ascribe to elements in the structure of the created world a finality which belongs only to Christ.

When we speak of culture in its broadest sense, we are speaking about the sum total of ways of living which shape (and also are shaped by) the continuing life of a group of human beings from generation to generation. We are speaking about the language which enables them to grasp, conceptualize, and communicate the reality of their world; about law, custom, and forms of social organization, including marriage, family, and nation; we are talking also about art, science, technology, and agriculture. These things shape the life of each member of the society. They are also shaped, modified, and developed from generation to generation by the members of the society. From the point of view of the individual member they are given as part of the tradition into which he is born and socialized. But they are not changeless absolutes.

If we are to grasp theologically the meaning of this "sum total of ways of living" from the point of view of the gospel, I think that we must do so by means of Paul's doctrine of the powers. If we take all of the references in the Pauline epistles both to "powers" and to the related words such as "rudiments" (*stoicheia*), it is clear that he is speaking of such things as the political order (Rom. 13), the law (Gal. 3:23–4:11), and the complex of rules and prohibitions that were current in the religious world of the eastern Mediterranean in the first century (such as in Col. 2:8–23). Paul speaks both positively and negatively about these things. Positively they have been created in Christ and for him (Col. 1:15–16). Negatively they have been disarmed by Christ on his cross (Col. 2:15). The powers of state, religion, law, and custom all conspired and combined to crucify Jesus. By this act they revealed their own insufficiency (I Cor. 2:8). They have been disarmed. They are not destroyed: they still exist. But their claim to absolute authority has been disallowed. They can no longer usurp the place that belongs to Christ alone. They can no longer separate

159

those who are in Christ from the direct presence of God himself in Jesus Christ (Rom. 8:38–39).

The "powers" are created in Christ and for Christ. They serve his purpose. They make human life possible. They provide the ordered framework within which it is possible for human freedom to develop. There is the orderly structure of nature, of the seasons, of day and night. There are the political orders and the rule of law. There is an accepted and understood language upon which we depend for learning, understanding, communicating. There are customs, traditions, norms for conduct upon which we rely to guide us in the actions we have to take from minute to minute. Without these given structures we could not begin to become human beings. We depend upon them to enable us to develop the very powers by which we can begin to question them.

They are given, but they are not changeless and absolute. They are part of the created order; they exist through the creative love and power of God. But that does not give them the status of changeless absolutes. Final authority belongs only to Christ. In his cross, where the powers combined to destroy him, Christ has established a place where we are related directly to God himself — a place, therefore, from which we have the freedom to judge, criticize, and challenge the powers. They still exist and perform their necessary function. But they must serve the purpose of Christ, and they are open to challenge by those who are in Christ, those to whom has been entrusted the secret of God's purpose to sum up all things, including all the powers, with Christ as their head (Eph. 1:10).

The bearing of this upon the question of conversion and culture is obvious. McGavran speaks of humanity as a vast mosaic of different cultures, each of which is "psychologically closed to the rest of the world." He says, therefore, that "adaptation of Christianity to the culture of each piece of the mosaic is crucially important." And it follows that "the true goal is to multiply *in every piece of the magnificent mosaic truly Christian churches which fit that piece,* are closely adapted to *its* culture, and recognized by *its* non-Christian neighbours as 'our kind of show.' "[7] What shall we say of this picture?

1. It is true that there are still living in some parts of the world communities which are in a large measure "psychologically closed to the rest of the world" and which have a common culture which is relatively static. But this description of human culture is not completely true even of such rare communities, and is wildly untrue of the vast majority of mankind. Certainly all human beings live in groups which share common cultural elements, but the following considerations will show how misleading the image of the mosaic can be.

(a) Every human community is changing. Some change more rapidly than others, but none is absolutely static. All the elements of culture, even in the most stable communities, are changing.

(b) Culture is not an ethically neutral entity, and cultural change cannot be a matter of ethical indifference. Some forms of social organization, of political order, of family life, of personal behavior, must be judged to be better than others in the light of the revelation in Christ of God's purpose for humanity. We may have to recognize that at certain times and places such institutions as slavery, polygamy, the dowry system, and the capitalist system exist as an integral part of the culture of a society and that the Christian convert cannot separate himself from them without ceasing to be part of that society. But we may also hold, nevertheless, that other ways of ordering the economic, marital, and political life of society are better and that there is an obligation upon Christians to seek to change these elements in a culture. The fact that something is part of a particular culture does not mean that the Christian can give it unconditional endorsement.

(c) In every community there are conservatives and

---

7. Donald McGavran, "The Dimensions of World Evangelization," Lausanne Congress strategy paper, 1974.

there are reformers, and there are different issues upon which the members of the society will take different sides. The danger inherent in all programs for the "indigenization" or "acculturation" of the gospel is that they involve the church with the conservative and backward-looking elements in the society. A study of the missionary history of the nineteenth century will show, on the other hand, that some of the foreign elements which were accepted by the converts from the missionaries were welcomed precisely *because* they made a break with the traditional culture and therefore came as reinforcement for younger elements in society who were impatient of old tradition. And where foreign missionaries, bearers of a culture considered (rightly or wrongly) to be "advanced," have tried to confine the "indigenous" church to the traditional language and culture of the past, they have been deeply and rightly resented. It is sufficient to mention the word "apartheid" to make the point.

(d) It is not true that the communities which are defined by a common culture are "psychologically closed to the rest of the world." Even in the remotest areas of the Amazon forests there is some mutual contact and some penetration of new ideas. And for the vast majority of the human race there is a continuous process of mutual influence between different groups. No group so absolutizes its own culture as to be immune to outside influences. Moreover — and this is still more important — a growing proportion of the human race lives in urban areas where each person is normally part of several cultural communities at the same time. An example may be taken from the city of Madras. There are probably almost a quarter of a million Christians in that city of three million inhabitants. McGavran (if I understand him) thinks that in the interests of effective evangelization the Christians should be organized in separate groups according to their caste origins. This, in his view, would make it easier and more natural for Hindus from the same caste to be converted. I leave aside, for the moment, the fact that most Christians in Madras would reject this on ethical grounds, believing that it is an essential part of Christian witness to affirm the unity of all in Christ. The question now is whether in fact caste is the most significant of the socializing factors in the life of a modern city like Madras. It is true that caste still plays an important part, but so do membership in a trade union and sharing in the same place of work. Granting as I do that the recipient of the gospel is the person in his community and not the person in isolation, I would still have to insist that in the Madras of today the working community is probably of more significance as the context of discipleship than is the traditional kinship group.

(e) These four considerations provide the context for a more biblical and theological argument. The picture of humanity as a vast mosaic of separate and unchanging cultures is misleading. All are interacting, all are changing, all are involved in the tension between the new and the old. The cultures cannot be absolutized over against the gospel. The cultures are elements in the created world which are subject to the rule of Christ, and the tension in which they live is part of the tension between the old creation and the new. Christ who is the head of the church is also the Lord of all cultures, and his purpose is that all shall be finally subject to him as head. It is not enough to speak of the numerical growth of the church within each "piece" of the mosaic, as though the latter was to remain to the end of time and as though the growth of the church was the ultimate purpose of God. We must seek the presence of the church within each part of the whole fabric of human culture, not as an end in itself, but as sign, instrument, and foretaste of God's purpose for all human culture. This means that the church is involved in and must take sides in the tensions which exist within each culture. It must so live, act, and speak within each culture that its words and its deeds and its life communicate in a way which can be understood the judgment of God upon that culture and his promise for it.

Clearly, therefore, one can speak of the path which the church must take as lying between two opposite dangers. The first danger is that the church may so conform its life and teaching to the culture that it no longer functions as the bearer of God's judgment and promise. It becomes simply the guardian and guarantor of the culture and fails to challenge it. The other danger is that the language and the life-style of the church should be such that they make no contact with the culture and become the language and life-style of a ghetto. Between these two extremes there is a wide spectrum of possibilities, parts of which have been explored in Richard Niebuhr's *Christ and Culture*. This classic work deals with the relation of church and culture within a single culture and does not raise the difficult and complicated questions which arise in the communication of the gospel from one culture to another. How, in seeking to preach the gospel to people of another culture, does the church find the proper path between a kind of accommodation which robs the gospel of its power to challenge traditional ways of life, and a kind of intransigence which either fails to communicate altogether or else alienates the converts from their culture? To this difficult question we must now turn.

2. (a) Any attempt to preach the gospel involves using the language spoken by the hearers. That language has been shaped by and has shaped their experience of life. It is the form in which they seek to grasp and make sense of the whole range of human experience. It embodies their beliefs about life and death, about sin and virtue, about guilt and forgiveness, about salvation and damnation, about soul and body, about time and eternity, about God and man. None of the language is "neutral"; it embodies beliefs to which its users are committed. These beliefs are not the same as those of the evangelist. Nevertheless the evangelist has no alternative except to use this language, doing the best he can to find words which will come as near as possible to creating in his hearers the belief he wants to share with them. When he has done his best to find idioms of speech, of life-style, of rite and liturgy which will most effectively embody the truth of the gospel, he will still have to recognize that these idioms, shaped as they are by a different set of beliefs, will distort the truth which they are employed to embody. There is no way of avoiding this fact.

(b) But in putting the matter in this way I have over-simplified it. I have left out of account the fact that the idioms of speech and conduct by which the evangelist grasps and expresses the gospel are themselves shaped by his culture. If he has had no experience of the sharp clash of cultures he may be unaware that this is so. He may suppose that the way he understands the gospel is the way it "really is." No doubt — especially if he is well instructed in the Reformed faith! — he will agree that his understanding of the gospel is always subject to correction by reference to the Bible. He will be confident that the Bible provides the sure standard of teaching and that it will confirm the truth of the gospel as he has tried to communicate it. And so the evangelist takes early steps to ensure that the Bible is translated and placed in the hands of the receptor community and that they are taught to read it.

(c) But the introduction of the Bible changes the situation. It is not long before the Bible begins to make its own impact on its readers in the receptor community. In its stories, its prayers, its ethical teachings, and above all in the figure of Jesus as he presents himself to fresh eyes through the medium of print, the readers are confronted with something which raises questions both about their traditional culture and about what has been offered to them by the evangelist as "Christianity." A three-cornered relationship is set up between the traditional culture, the "Christianity" of the missionary, and the Bible. The stage is set for a complex and unpredictable evolution both in the culture of the receptor community and in that of the missionary. As an illustration of the former one could point to the massive development of the so-called African Independent churches. These have developed by a process of ferment, renewal, and schism within the churches established by Western missions, and the studies of David Barrett[8] have demonstrated an extremely close correlation between the

---

8. David Barrett, *Schism and Renewal in Africa* (Nairobi: Oxford Univ. Press, 1968).

formation of the independent churches and the availability of the Scriptures in the languages of the communities concerned. That is to say that the Bible has operated as an independent source of criticism directed both against the Christianity of the missionaries and against the traditional culture of the tribe. The Independent churches are marked not only by the rejection of certain aspects of Western Christianity but also by an equally sharp rejection of elements in the traditional African culture. Werner Hoerschelmann has documented comparable movements in South India.[9]

It must be admitted that the Western churches which have sent missions to Asia and Africa have remained very largely unaffected by the development which I have described because their missionaries have operated at a distance from the sending churches and on the extreme periphery of their consciousness. But like others who have spent long periods in foreign missionary service, I have to bear witness that the experience of living for most of four decades as part of an Indian church has made me acutely aware of the cultural conditioning of the Christianity in which I was nurtured, and of the culture-bound character of many of the assumptions which are unquestioned by English Christians. I shall have to revert to this point later.

(d) I said that this triangle of forces made up by the culture, the invading culture, and the Bible sets the stage for a complicated and unpredictable evolution. This is no uniform pattern. Sometimes the impact of the experience of salvation in Jesus Christ is such that questions concerning the traditional culture drop into insignificance. They are regarded as *adiaphora*. Only after some time do the converts begin to draw from their new experience critical questions about their traditional culture. More often the first response is a strong reaction against the traditional culture. It is "the world" which is still in the power of evil. The new life in Christ is so absolutely new that the old must be put away.

---

9. Werner Hoerschelmann, *Christliche Gurus* (Frankfurt, 1977).

At this stage it is the Christianity of the invading culture that is accepted and welcomed. The message is so closely linked with the messenger who brought it that there is no desire to separate them. There is a sharp rejection of elements in the old culture which, even if not evil in themselves (such as music, drama, and visual art), are felt to be evil because of their association with the rejected world view.

After the passage of some years, often in the second or third generation of the church, a new situation arises. The church has now become so much at home in a new thought-world that the old no longer poses a threat. The old culture has been for these Christians desacralized. Its music, art, dance, and social customs are no longer feared because of their pagan associations; in fact they begin to be prized as part of the world which God loves and which he has given to men. The church begins for the first time to think about the relation of Christ to culture. It begins to experiment with the variety of possible models for this relation. In some cases, as for example in many of the South Pacific Islands, a new *Corpus Christianum* comes into existence. There is a practical identification of church and society, and Christ is seen as the one who harmonizes and reconciles the old culture. In other situations, especially where the church is a small minority, there is a strong effort to reverse the alienation from local culture which marked the first conversions and to approach the older culture in a spirit of acceptance and openness. The tendency then will be to search for christological models which can be accommodated within the thought-world of the older culture. And again there will be movements of renewal which often take the form of a sharp attack upon elements both in the church and in the old culture. There is an almost infinite variety of different situations, and none of them is static.

(e) It is already clear that we have moved a long way from the simple picture of a culturally uncontaminated gospel being planted in a series of culturally isolated, stable, and homogeneous communities. In fact the Christianity which the missionary brings is already conditioned by his own culture, and the community to which he brings it is a changing entity exposed to contact without and tension within. I have suggested that within the receptor community there is a complex evolution determined by three factors: the traditional culture, the Christianity of the missionary, and the witness of the Bible. But it is clear that this also is far from being the full picture. In the modern world all human communities, with very few exceptions, are exposed to cultural influences of many kinds from one another. We do inhabit one single planet, and we are more and more closely crowded together. The three-cornered relation of which I have spoken is not isolated from this contact. Each of these patterns of development is part of the vast and infinitely complex pattern of intercultural influence on a global scale. And the Christian communities within each culture, being bound together in the growing fellowship of the ecumenical movement, have to be open both to the cultures in which they participate as members of nations, citizens of cities, workers, thinkers, etc., and also open to the Christian testimony of those who inhabit other cultural worlds but share a common allegiance to Jesus Christ. This openness to Christians of other cultures and the experience of ecumenical fellowship which it makes possible, will provide a continuing critique of the ways in which the church within any culture is related to that culture. All will acknowledge in principle that the gospel cannot be completely domesticated within any culture. The Christ who is presented in Scripture for our believing is Lord over all cultures, and his purpose is to unite all of every culture to himself in a unity which transcends without negating the diversities of culture. But, as we well know, the Scriptures alone do not suffice to prevent us from the attempt to domesticate him within our cultures. The bewildering variety of ways in which Jesus has been portrayed by Christian artists who have the same Bible in their hands but belong to different cultures is sufficient evidence of the cultural conditioning of our reading of Scripture. We need the witness of Christians of other cultures to correct our culturally conditioned understanding of Scripture.

Starting from the simple core of a missionary preaching the gospel for the first time in a community which has not previously heard it, I have moved on to a picture of the church as a global fellowship in which the same three-cornered pattern of relationships is continuously developing. At the level of the local church one can picture an ideal situation in which there is at the same time full openness to the local culture, to the Scriptures, and to the witness of other Christians in the ecumenical family. The day-to-day worship and work and witness of the local church has to be developed in relationship to all of these in such a way that it becomes credible to the inhabitants of the local culture as sign, instrument, and foretaste of that one universal reign of God which is the true origin and goal of this and every human culture. It must communicate in the idiom of that culture both the divine good which sustains it and the divine purpose which judges it and summons it to become what it is not yet. At the world level the corresponding picture would be of a fellowship of Christian churches open to and rooted in all the cultures of mankind within which they are severally placed, and so renewing its life through ever-fresh obedience to Christ as presented in the Scriptures that it becomes an increasingly credible sign, instrument, and foretaste of God's reign over all nations and all things.

The contemporary ecumenical movement is a frail, limited, and stumbling move towards such a vision of the universal fellowship of churches. I shall say something of its limitations in a moment. But first it is proper to acknowledge with thankfulness that within these limitations it is a real movement towards this goal. Like multitudes of others who have shared in ecumenical meetings I have experienced the strain and even contradiction between different understandings of the gospel which have arisen out of different cultural situations. I have been tempted to ask whether the contradiction was not total, whether we were really speaking of the same reality when we used our different languages about Jesus and the gospel. But I have also known again and again, as others have, the experience of finding — as we prayed together, studied the Scriptures together, and listened to one another's experiences of Christ — that there was and is one Lord Jesus Christ to whom we are in our different ways bearing witness, and that he has indeed bound us together in himself in bonds which are stronger than those which bind us to our several cultures. It is out of such experiences that we return to our local churches with fresh awareness of the sharpness of the Word of God as it is addressed to our own cultures.

But with these thankful and positive statements I must also speak of the limitation of the contemporary ecumenical movement. And here I am not speaking of the limitations which beset any movement because of the weakness and sinfulness of those who participate. I am referring to a very specific defect which has far-reaching implications for the present discussion of church and culture. The contemporary ecumenical movement was born among the churches which share in common the culture that has developed in western Europe and North America in the past centuries and which has undergone enormously rapid transformation since the Age of Reason in the eighteenth century. All its work is conducted in the languages of western Europe. Only those who have had long training in the methods of thinking, of study and research, and of argument which have been developed in western Europe can share in its work. These ways of thinking have become so dominant throughout the world during the past two centuries that it is very difficult for those who have never known anything else to realize that they are only one of the possible ways in which men and women have found it possible to make sense of their experience. I may perhaps be able to make the point clear by the following illustration. Anyone who has lived within the Tamil churches knows that there are rich resources of living Christian faith and experience embodied in the continuing stream of Tamil Christian lyrical poetry, a stream which has flowed for a century and a half and is still flowing strongly. The people who write and read and sing these lyrics do not take any part in the work of the ecumenical movement. Their lyrics cannot be translated into a European language without losing their power and beauty. The world of thought, the concepts through which they capture and express the deepest Christian experiences are not those which appear in the documents of ecumenical meetings. Only those Tamil Christians who have undergone a long and rigorous training in Western methods of study, argument, and experiment can participate in these meetings. It is almost impossible for them to communicate in these meetings what is most vital and powerful in the life of the churches from which they come. I am sure that similar testimony could be given about the Christian culture of many parts of Asia, Africa, and the Pacific.

For those who have never lived in any other cultural world than that of the contemporary West it is very hard to see that theirs is only one of the tribal cultures of mankind. They are inclined to see it simply as the "modern scientific world view." It is the only way in which systematic and rigorous thinking can be done. Anything else has to be translated into these forms before it can be seriously studied. Even so sensitive a thinker as Hans Küng advises the theologians of the great world religions that they will have to "develop scientific theologies in the modern sense" before we can have a really fruitful dialogue among the world faiths.[10] Because of this cultural dominance of one set of cultural patterns the whole ecumenical movement is severely limited, and Christians who inhabit this cultural world do not receive from Christians of other cultures the correction which they need. It is true that there is at present some enthusiasm for "third world theologies," but these are normally theologies written in the language of Europe and (it must be frankly said) are too often echoes of earlier phases

---

10. Hans Küng, *On Being a Christian* (Garden City, N.Y.: Doubleday, 1976), p. 105.

of European thought — Marxist, Hegelian, or other. The real power of Asian and African Christianity does not lie in these productions. It lies in the very heart of the Christian life and practice of peoples who naturally live out their Christian faith in the idiom of their own culture and who continue to win their own people to Christ's service through this witness. Theologians of the "older" churches have often expressed their anxiety lest the "younger" churches of Asia and Africa should yield to the temptation of syncretism and should develop theologies too closely shaped by their traditional cultures. Just because of the total dominance of European culture in the ecumenical movement there has seldom been any awareness among Western theologians of the extent to which their own theologies have been the result of a failure to challenge the assumptions of their own culture, and because theologians of the younger churches have been compelled to adopt this culture as the precondition of participation in the ecumenical movement they have not been in a position to present the really sharp challenge which should be addressed to the theologies of the Western churches. The point which I have to make in the final section of this chapter will perhaps illustrate this contention.

3. I have described the interaction between gospel and culture as a continually developing relationship within a triangular field of which the three points are the local culture, the ecumenical fellowship representing the witness of Christians from other cultures, and the Scriptures as embodying the given revelation with its center and focus in the person of Jesus Christ. In discussion of these matters with colleagues who belong to the cultural world which understands itself to be committed to the modern scientific world view I have found that while there is no question about the first two points of this triangle, there is considerable questioning of the third. In other words, the modern Western theologian will fully recognize the necessity for openness to and dialogue with the local culture, and for the ecumenical dialogue with the whole Christian fellowship. The question

will be whether, and in what sense, the Scriptures can be said to function as a third and independent party in this development. When such a place is claimed for Scripture in a discussion within the modern scientific world, three objections are likely to be raised.

(a) The Bible itself represents the experiences of one particular culture or complex of cultures. The New Testament speaks the languages and uses the models of a particular time and place in human history. It is no Switzerland among the cultures of the world, no "neutral zone," no "non-aligned state." It arises out of the experience of a people, or a group of peoples, among all the peoples of mankind. It is indelibly marked by their cultural peculiarities and it is embodied in their languages. How, then, can it be absolutized, given an authority over the products of other cultures?

(b) Within the New Testament itself there is a variety of interpretations of the gospel. Some appear to be shaped by models drawn from the Old Testament, some from Iranian mythology, some from the world of Greek philosophy. How can this collection of varied models, all related to particular temporary and local forms of culture, provide criteria by which all future models, based on the whole range of human culture, may be tested?

(c) Critical study of the New Testament, using the tools of modern historical research, has led many scholars to believe that it is impossible to have any knowledge of the life, character, and teaching of Jesus sufficiently reliable to provide a criterion for judging the future developments. We cannot, it is said, be sure how far the material in the New Testament represents the character and message of Jesus himself and how far it represents the beliefs of the primitive church.

These questions obviously raise issues which could only be adequately discussed in a series of volumes, but the present discussion requires some attention to them because they obviously affect the integrity and authority of the Christian mission.

(a) It is, of course, unquestionable that the Bible has its locus in one particular part of the whole fabric of human culture. This fact is indeed the constant horizon of the biblical narrative from the time it is said God chose the clan of Eber from among all the seventy nations that made up the human family. Here is a primitive expression of the dogma, which is central to the Christian tradition, that God has chosen one people among all the people to be the unique bearer of his saving purpose for all nations. In contemporary Western culture this is confronted by the statement that it is impossible to believe that one among all the cultures should have this unique position. The alleged impossibility rests upon another dogma regarding the meaning of human experience. Here two different dogmatic systems confront one another, and I know of no set of axioms more fundamental than either of them, on the basis of which it would be possible to demonstrate the truth of one of these dogmas and the falsity of the other. According to one dogma, world history is in some sense a coherent whole, and it is therefore possible to affirm that certain events have a unique significance for the entire story. According to the other dogma, there are no events which have such unique significance and therefore no universally valid affirmation can be made about the meaning of history as a whole. The Christian affirmation about the unique significance of these events is a dogmatic statement made as part of the total faith-commitment to Jesus as Lord. The contrary affirmation rests upon a different dogma which belongs to the dominant "myth" of contemporary Western culture. Here the question at issue is not one of "translation" from one cultural world to another, but the clash of ultimate faith-commitment.

However, the acknowledgment that this particular part of the whole fabric of human culture has a unique place still leaves open the question about the manner in which this uniqueness is to be interpreted. Does it mean that the cultural forms of the Semitic world have authority over all other cultural forms? Are those who accept the uniqueness and finality of God's revelation of himself in a Jewish male of the first century obliged to accept the cultural forms in which that revelation was given? Plainly no, for the New Testament itself records the debate which arose within the primitive community at the point when the testimony about Jesus moved from a Jewish into a Greek culture. The answers given to the question were not clear-cut, for the "decrees" recorded in Acts 15:29 include purely Semitic elements which could not be and have not been accepted as permanently valid. But the answers given do make plain that incorporation into the community of Jesus Christ did not mean acceptance of the cultural world in which Jesus himself had lived and which he had accepted. Jesus himself apparently never questioned the law of circumcision. The decisive mark of membership in the new community was nothing definable in terms of culture; it was a reality — apparently quite unmistakable — recognized as the presence of the Holy Spirit.

With this I have already moved into the second of my three questions, that of the variety of voices with which the New Testament speaks of Jesus.

(b) The fact that the New Testament contains not one but several interpretations of Christ prompts the following reflections:

(*i*) The first is a negative one. There is a variety, but not an unlimited variety, of Christologies in the New Testament. In determining which of the traditions regarding Jesus should be included in the canon and which should be excluded, the church was guided by the belief that the name of Jesus referred to a real man who had lived at a known time and in a known place, and that therefore traditions must be verified against the testimony of original witnesses or of those who were related to the original witnesses by a continuous tradition of public teaching. By this test certain interpretations of the person and teaching of Jesus had to be rejected. Those which were accepted, varied as they are, were united by the fact that they were judged to be reliable reports about the same person. The inclusion of a variety of differing accounts, and the absence of any attempt to iron

175

out these differences so as to create a single picture, is evidence of the fact that the controlling factor was the actual person who had lived — not the doctrines about him.

(ii) The second reflection is positive. It is important for a faithful doing of Christian theology that we should affirm and insist that the New Testament contains not one Christology but several. This is not an unfortunate defect to be regretted or concealed. It is, on the contrary, of the essence of the matter because it makes clear the fact that Christology is always to be done *in via,* at the interface between the gospel and the cultures which it meets on its missionary journey. It is of the essence of the matter that Jesus was not concerned to leave as the fruit of his work a precise verbatim record of everything he said and did, but that he was concerned to create a community which would be bound to him in love and obedience, learn discipleship even in the midst of sin and error, and be his witnesses among all peoples. The varied Christologies to be discovered in the New Testament reflect the attempts of that community to say who Jesus is in the terms of the different cultures within which they bore witness to him. If there were to be discovered in the New Testament one definitive Christology framed in the *ipsissima verba* of Jesus himself, the consequence would be that the gospel would be forever bound absolutely to the culture of first-century Palestine. The New Testament would have to be regarded as untranslatable, as is the Qur'an among Muslims. We would be dealing with a different kind of religion altogether. The *variety* of Christologies actually to be found in the New Testament is part of the fundamental witness to the nature of the gospel: it points to the *destination* of the gospel in all the cultures of mankind. The *unity* of the New Testament, the fact that it contains, not every Christology, but only those which were judged to be faithful to the original testimony, reflects the *origin* of the gospel in the one unique person of Jesus.

(iii) These two reflections, negative and positive, lead to the affirmation that the New Testament, read as it must always be in the context of the Old, provides us, in the

variety and unity of its interpretation of Jesus, with the *canon* — the guide and regulator of our doing of Christology. It shows us that Christology must always be something which is *in via,* incomplete, but it shows us that the road has a real starting point in the historic fact of Jesus Christ who lived, taught, died, and rose again under Pontius Pilate; that it has a real destination in the universal confession of this Jesus as Lord; and that the two conditions for the journey are faithful confession within the varied cultures, and faithful mutual openness within the ecumenical fellowship.

(c) This brings us, however, to the third of the questions which modern critical study of the New Testament poses: do we, in fact, have such reliable knowledge of "the historic fact of Christ" as would enable us to speak thus of a known starting point for the journey of Christology? Obviously it is impossible to discuss such a large and much debated question here; it is, however, necessary to draw attention to one point in the debate which is relevant to the discussion.

I have already sought to show (in Chapter 7) that the application of modern methods of critical historical research to the contents of the New Testament involves two distinct issues from the point of view of the present discussion. On the one hand it involves the use of greatly improved tools for examining the origins of each tradition and the factors which have shaped its formation and influenced its transmission. But it involves also the presuppositions which control the use of these tools. Every attempt to write history involves, as I have already argued, assumptions about what is significant, and therefore assumptions about the ultimate meaning of the story which alone can give significance to any part of it. But the question of the ultimate meaning of history is the question of one's ultimate faith-commitment. The question has to be pressed whether the skepticism of many Western theologians about the possibility of a reliable knowledge of the "Jesus of history" does not arise from an uncritical acceptance of the implicit faith-commitment which has dominated the culture of the (admittedly large and influential) tribe to which they have belonged since the Enlightenment of the eighteenth century.

The body of the New Testament writing was formed within a community which believed that the ultimate meaning of the whole human story had been declared in the total fact of Jesus Christ as the first witnesses had known him. Within the limitations of the historical methods available to them within their culture, they sought to create and hand on a record which was faithful to the original testimony of those who had known Jesus in the flesh and who were the witnesses of his resurrection. The controlling belief which shaped the selection and handling of the material was that in Jesus the meaning of the whole of history is revealed. Within this perspective the Jesus of history *is* the Christ of faith.

It is of course possible to hold a completely different view of the meaning of the story or to hold (as the Indian tradition has generally done) that the story has no meaning. It is clear that a momentous shift took place about two hundred years ago in the thinking of the people of western Europe about the way in which the story was to be understood. The idea of progress, that is to say the idea that the meaning of the story is to be found in the progressive mastery of man's reason over the powers of nature and over tradition and social structures inherited from the past, seems to have become operative in the European mind during the eighteenth century. When history is understood in this way, it is obvious that the story about Jesus cannot have the decisive place. In fact, from the period of the Enlightenment to the present day, world history is normally taught in schools and universities from a point of view which puts into the decisive place such things as the development of modern science, the industrial revolution, and the evolution of modern forms of political order. The story about Jesus may still have a central place in "religious instruction," but it will have only a marginal place in "world history." It retains a place in the sphere of personal religion, but it does not determine the way history as a whole is understood.

It is natural that a scholar operating within the assumption of modern European culture, when he comes to study the biblical records as history, will bring to them these assumptions. His work as a historian will be governed by assumptions other than those which are expressed in the hymns and prayers used in church. He will have to try to understand Jesus from the standpoint of a "modern critical historian," and it will inevitably follow that the historical Jesus whom he discovers will be a different figure from the Christ of the Christian faith. It is not that there are two different realities. There is only one Jesus and only one set of records. The difference lies in the prior assumptions which are brought to the study of the records.

Of course, it has to be added immediately that the Christ of faith is seen very differently from different cultural perspectives. I have already fully acknowledged this. I have affirmed my belief (part of the fundamental commitment upon which the whole mission of the church rests) that these different perceptions are perceptions of one real person who is decisive for all that it means to be human. I have insisted that these different perceptions are never to be absolutized but have always to be subject to correction within the believing, worshiping, serving, and witnessing fellowship of churches. But — and here is the essential point for the moment — I have argued that this ecumenical fellowship is distorted by its dependence almost entirely upon one set of cultural models, namely, those of the Western world. Consequently the necessary ecumenical correction is not applied to the theology that arises within this culture. Its practitioners find it hard to recognize that the "modern scientific view of history" is only one among a number of possible ways of looking at history. They find it difficult to recognize the culturally conditioned nature of their fundamental presuppositions. They are therefore tempted to absolutize these presuppositions and to relativize the traditional testimony about Jesus. It is the urgent need of the hour that the ecumenical fellowship of churches should become so released from its present dependence upon one set of cultural forms that it can provide the place wherein we are able to do theology in the only way that it can be done properly — by learning with increasing clarity to confess the one Lord Jesus Christ as alone having absolute authority and therefore to recognize the relativity of all the cultural forms within which we try to say who he is.

10

The Gospel among the Religions

I

AT THE OUTSET of this discussion, in speaking of the question of authority, I affirmed my belief that the Christian mission rests upon a total and unconditional commitment to Jesus Christ as the one in whom all authority inheres. This initial affirmation has governed the whole discussion. It is now necessary to face the difficult questions which arise when this commitment is brought into contact with other unconditional commitments of the same kind. In the title of this chapter the word "religion" is intended to denote all those commitments which, in the intention of their adherents, have an overriding authority over all other commitments and provide the framework within which all experience is grasped and all ideas are judged. In this sense the word will include an ideology such as Marxism which functions, both for the committed individual and for societies under Marxist control, as such an ultimate commitment.

I realize the word "religion" is a notoriously difficult one. It can be used to describe any system of belief and practice which implies some sort of transcendence of the experience of the senses, in which case it becomes too vague to be useful. It is sometimes used as if it referred to beliefs

181

and practices concerning God and the immortal soul — in which case it is too narrow, for it excludes the original message of the Buddha. I am using it to refer to that which has final authority for a believer or a society, both in the sense that it determines his scale of values and in the sense that it provides the models, the basic patterns through which the believer grasps and organizes his experience. When the word is used in this way it follows that it will include ideologies as well as what are usually called religions. It also becomes necessary to point out that what a man calls "his religion" may in fact be other than the ultimately authoritative factor in his thinking and acting. It is, for example, obvious that a person may be a Christian and yet limit the operation of his Christian commitment to a restricted field (for example, to the private and domestic life) while his ultimate commitment is to some other way of understanding experience, to his traditional tribal "myth" or, in the case of contemporary Western man, to the modern scientific world view. In this case his commitment to Christ will be conditioned by his commitment to the overrriding "myth," and the latter will be his real religion.

I am concerned with the issues which arise from the meeting of different and discordant commitments which are for the participants their ultimate commitments. This means that I shall not be discussing the enterprise usually known in English as "comparative religion" or in German as *Religionswissenschaft*. This increasingly prestigious academic discipline was defined by one of its great pioneers as "a science of religion based on an impartial and truly scientific comparison of all, or at all events, of the most important religions of mankind."[1] This enterprise, the history of which has been magisterially surveyed in the book of Eric Sharpe just quoted, is outside of my discussion here because it does not envisage the possibility with which I am now concerned, namely, the possibility of the meeting of

---

1. Max Müller, *Introduction to the Science of Religion* (1873), quoted in Eric Sharpe, *Comparative Religion* (London: Duckworth, 1975), p. xi.

different ultimate commitments. For Max Müller and his successors it is clear that the ultimate commitment is to the scientific method as the clue to the apprehension of truth. In the passage just quoted, Müller calls upon the scientific community "to take possession of this new territory in the name of true science." This is the confident language of the pioneer missionary who has not yet found it necessary to consider the truth-claims of the tribal myths and religions of the natives. The possibility is not envisaged that the very foundations of "true science" might be called into question by one of the religions to be studied. There is no meeting, no encounter, no mutual challenge: there is only the triumphant advance of "true science" into unevangelized territory. The missionary has not yet become aware of the fact that his own vision of the truth is, from another point of view, only the dominant "myth" of the tribe which happens at that moment (the end of the nineteenth century) to have acquired unchallenged dominance over most of the world. His "scientific objectivity" conceals from him the whole set of models by which he organizes and grasps his experience, and it is to these that his ultimate commitment is given.

A more subtle and much more ancient way of approaching the variety of religions is embodied in the oft-told Indian tale of the king who invited a number of blind men to his court, put an elephant in their midst, and asked them to say what it was. Their varied answers were intended not only to amuse the courtiers but also to teach them that the diverse religions of the world are but the gropings of blind men after a truth much too great for any human mind to grasp. The story aptly expresses the basic philosophy of the Vedanta, namely, that ultimate reality is not a matter of knowledge (which implies the dualism of known and unknown) but of the realization of the identity of the eternal self and the self of the whole universe — the identity of *atman* and *brahman*. The ultimate reality can therefore only be indicated by negatives: *neti neti* ("not that"). The whole point of the story is that the blind men represent the religions, but the king, who is not blind, represents the one who has attained to this realization and who therefore "sees." Once again, there is no encounter. There is no possibility that one of the religions might call in question the interpretation of the mystical experience on which the whole philosophy of the Vedanta rests. The story implies simply that the philosophy of the Vedanta is that which corresponds to reality and that all else is blindness.

It is understandable that anyone faced with the clashing diversity of religious commitments should seek some basis for unity among them, or at least some agreed common framework. The difficulty is that we are dealing here with *ultimate* commitments, and the basis which I accept can only be *my* commitment. There have been many attempts to find a basis which all could accept, but none of them escapes this necessity. Professor John Hick has proposed a "Copernican revolution" in theology which would solve the problem of interreligious understanding by means of "a shift from the dogma that Christianity is at the centre to the realisation that it is God who is at the centre, and that all the religions of mankind, including our own, serve and revolve round him."[2] Clearly there is a logical fallacy in comparing this proposal to the shift from a Ptolemaic to a Copernican view of the solar system. The sun, the planets, and the earth are all objects capable of investigation by the same methods of observation; they are equally objects of sense-perception. God and the religions are not objects in the same class. If the analogy of the Copernican revolution is to be applied to the relation of Christianity and the other religions without logical fallacy, then like must be compared with like. God is not accessible to observation in the same sense in which the world religions are, and we have no frame of reference within which we can compare God as he really is with God as conceived in the world religions. The two realities which are accessible and comparable are God as I conceive him and God as the world religions conceive him. What claims to be a

---

2. John Hick, *God and the Universe of Faith* (New York: St. Martin's Press, 1973), p. 131.

model for the unity of religions turns out in fact to be the claim that one theologian's conception of God is the reality which is the central essence of all religions. This is the trap into which every program for the unity of the religions is bound to fall. There is no real encounter. Hick's conception of God simply is the truth and there is no possibility that one of the world's religions can challenge it.

I have said that it is very understandable that we should look for some point of view which would enable us to bring together these clashing commitments in a single framework. It is understandable, but we have to face the fact that it is impossible. The framework which I devise or discern is my ultimate commitment or else it cannot function in the way intended. As such a commitment, it must defend its claim to truth over against other claims to truth. I have no standpoint except the point where I stand. The claim that I have is simply the claim that mine is the standpoint from which it is possible to discern the truth that relativizes all truth. That claim is the expression of the ultimate commitment which is my real religion.

If this argument is valid, it follows that the Christian will meet his friend and neighbor of another faith as one who is committed to Jesus Christ as his ultimate authority, who openly acknowledges this commitment, and seeks to understand and to enter into dialogue with his partner of another commitment on that basis.

In his Younghusband Lecture, "Christian Theology and Inter-Religious Dialogue," John Hick has commented on this approach to dialogue. He writes that theological dialogue between the religions takes place within a spectrum which ranges between two opposite conceptions of its nature.

> At one extreme there is purely confessional dialogue in which each partner witnesses to his own faith, convinced that his has absolute truth whilst his partner's has only relative truth. At the other extreme is truth-seeking dialogue in which each is conscious that Transcendent Being is infinitely greater than his own limited vision of it, and in which they accordingly seek to

share their vision in the hope that each may be helped towards a fuller awareness of the Divine Reality before which they both stand.[3]

The Christian who enters into dialogue on the basis of his own "confession" must recognize that others will do the same. But each participant will see the other religions from the point of view of his own. Each one "has the impression of standing at the centre of a world of meaning and with all other faiths dispersed around its periphery,"[4] and of course from a global point of view there is a plurality of such "circles of faith." In spite of some refinements of this confessional stance (which we shall discuss later) Hick is concerned that this stance is unfruitful, as it can only end either "in conversion or in a hardening of differences."[5] Therefore "Christianity must move emphatically from the confessional to the truth-seeking stance in dialogue."[6] In the second part of his paper Hick discusses the impact of the rise of modern science on Christianity, and its probable impact upon the other religions in the coming decades. He traces the rise of modern science to the awakening of the European mind from its "dogmatic slumbers" under the influence of the rediscovered idea of the Graeco-Roman civilization. It has forced Christianity to make major transformations, and it will have a similar impact upon the other world religions. And in fact the uniqueness of Christianity consists in the fact that it has "given birth to the modern mentality."[7] Christianity must now join with the other "great streams of faith within which human life is lived"[8] to find answers to the problems with which modern science and technology confront us all.

Hick asks the Christian to "move emphatically from the

---

3. John Hick, "Christian Theology and Inter-Religious Dialogue," in *World Faiths*, no. 103 (Autumn 1977), pp. 2–19.
4. Ibid., p. 4.
5. Ibid., p. 7.
6. Ibid., p. 11.
7. Ibid., p. 18.
8. Ibid., p. 19.

confessional to the truth-seeking stance in dialogue." The latter stance is indicated in the affirmation that "Transcendent Being is infinitely greater than (one's) own limited view of it." The former stance might be indicated by such an affirmation as "Jesus Christ is Lord of all." Each of these is an affirmation of faith. Neither is an assertion of omniscience. The Christian will also say, "Jesus Christ is infinitely greater than my limited view of him." In these respects the two affirmations are analogous. Both are — or can be — made by people who are seriously seeking the truth. The difference lies in the way truth is to be sought, the clues which are to be followed, the models by which it is to be grasped, and the weight which is to be given to different kinds of evidence. The "confessional" stance implies that truth is to be found in a life of obedient discipleship to Jesus Christ as he is to be known through a life lived in the community of disciples, in faithfulness to the tradition about him, and in openness to all the truth which may be discovered in the history of the human race. The basic commitment is to a historic person and to historic deeds. It rests upon a life lived, upon deeds done, upon events in history.

The other stance takes as its point of reference Transcendent Being. (The capital letters are presumably to be taken seriously.) This is of course not a recorded event in history. It is an idea difficult for one not trained in philosophy to grasp. "Transcendent" is an adjective which literally refers to the position of something above or beyond something else. "Being" is a verbal noun from the verb "to be" which normally only has meaning in association with a subject. The idea of "being" which is devoid of any subject, that is, devoid of any reference to something which *is,* seems for most people to be very difficult to grasp. A person untrained in philosophy may be forgiven for asking whether "Being" which is not being anything is not a figment of the imagination. The phrase "Transcendent Being" is one which can be used meaningfully in Hick's lecture because he is addressing people who are familiar with the long history of philosophical idealism. His statement is in fact an affirmation of his faith that it is in this tradition that truth is to be sought and found. It is entirely right and proper for him to affirm this faith and to defend it against other views of how truth is to be sought. But two points must surely be made.

First, it is not obvious that the very abstract mental concept, which only a very small number of philosophers trained in certain disciplines is capable of grasping, is a more reliable starting point for the adventure of truth-seeking than is the fact of Jesus Christ. Every attempt to form a coherent understanding of the whole human situation starts out from an initial act of faith. There is no possibility of knowing anything except on the basis of something which is, at least provisionally, taken for granted. In this respect the Christian believer and the idealist philosopher share the same human predicament. My point is that I know of no basis, no axiom, no necessity of thought which requires me to believe that a historic person and a series of historic events provide a less reliable starting point for the adventure of knowing than does the highly sophisticated mental construct of a philosopher. Second, and more serious, Hick uses the words "confessional" and "truth-seeking" to define the two stances. The implication is that those who take the confessional stance are not seekers after truth. This is surely a very serious matter. One cannot enter into real dialogue if one begins by denying the intellectual integrity of one's partner. Under the guise of openness and teachability, Hick is in fact asserting that his own presuppositions are the way to arrive at truth and are acceptable as such, whereas those of the Christian are not. It is in line with this that Hick regularly uses the word "dogma" to describe the basic presuppositions of Christians, while his own basic presuppositions are simply a transcript of reality as it is. Among many examples I will cite only the key phrase already quoted from *God and the Universe of Faiths:* "A shift from the dogma that Christianity is at the centre to

188

the *realisation* that it is God who is at the centre."⁹ The
Christian who takes part in dialogue cannot accept as a basis
for dialogue the view that his commitment to Jesus Christ
precludes him from seeking the truth and that he can only
qualify as a seeker after truth by adopting the commitment
of the idealist. On the basis which Hick proposes, there is in
fact no encounter between the faiths. It is eliminated at the
outset by the dogma that only one set of presuppositions can
provide the conditions of truth-seeking.

The further argument of the lecture makes this still
more clear. The shift in European thought which displaced
the Christian world view with patterns of thought derived
from Greek philosophy is described by Hick as Europe's
"awakening from its dogmatic slumbers." The "scientific
outlook" which has dispelled these slumbers is thus seen as
the basis upon which all the religions, including Christianity, are judged. In this section of the paper Hick unwit-
tingly illustrates precisely the pattern which he has earlier
described in condemning the "confessional stance." As one
committed to the "modern scientific world view" he also is
"standing at the centre of a world of meanings, with all
other faiths dispersed around its periphery," and he thus
exemplifies his own observation that the inhabitants of each
of the "circles of faith . . . all live under the same impression
of their own unique centrality."¹⁰ There is no suggestion that the "modern scientific world view" is open to
radical challenge from the standpoint of another faith.
There is no recognition of the fact that this view is only one
of the many ways in which men and women can grasp their
experience of the world. There is therefore no dialogue, no
encounter. There is only the monologue of the one who is
awake addressed to those who are presumed to be asleep, or
who have not yet wholly roused themselves from their
"dogmatic slumbers."

9. Hick, *God and the Universe of Faiths,* p. 131.
10. Hick, "Christian Theology and Inter-Religious Dialogue," pp. 4–5.

189

There is a sad irony about the fact that these things can be written just at the time when the foundations of the modern scientific world view seem to be crumbling, when the culture of the Western white man which dominated the world fifty years ago is visibly sinking into nihilism. It is surely becoming clear now that Greek rationalism can no more provide the ultimate basis for society in the twentieth century than it did in the third and fourth and that if the precious values of modern Western culture are to be saved from destruction it will be on the basis of resources drawn from another source. That source will be an ultimate faith-commitment which is honest enough to recognize that it is one among the possible commitments. At the risk of wearisome reiteration I must repeat the simple truth that no standpoint is available to any man except the point where he stands; that there is no platform from which one can claim to have an "objective" view which supersedes all the "subjective" faith-commitments of the world's faiths; that every man must take his stand on the floor of the arena, on the same level with every other, and there engage in the real encounter of ultimate commitment with those who, like him, have staked their lives on their vision of the truth.

I conclude this part of the argument, then, with the affirmation that the Christian goes to meet his neighbor of another religion on the basis of his commitment to Jesus Christ. There is no dichotomy between "confession" and "truth-seeking." His confession is the starting point of his truth-seeking. He meets his partner with the expectation and hope of hearing more of truth. But inevitably he will seek to grasp the new truth offered him by means of those ways of thinking and judging and valuing which he has already learned and tested. The presuppositions which shape his thinking will be those which he draws from the gospel. This must be quite explicit. He cannot agree that the position of final authority can be taken by anything other than the gospel — either by a philosophical system, or by mystical experience, or by the requirements of national and global unity. Confessing Christ — incarnate, crucified, and risen — as the true light and the true life, he cannot accept any other alleged authority as having right of way over this. He cannot regard the revelation given in Jesus as one of a type or as requiring interpretation by means of categories based on other ways of understanding the totality of experience. Jesus is for the believer the source from whom his understanding of the totality of experience is drawn and therefore the criterion by which other ways of understanding are judged.

In this respect the Christian will be in the same position as his partners in dialogue. The Hindu, the Muslim, the Buddhist, the Marxist — each has his distinctive interpretation of other religions, including Christianity, and the faith of each provides the basis of his own understanding of the totality of experience and, therefore, the criterion by which other ways of understanding, including that of the Christian, are judged. The integrity and fruitfulness of the interfaith dialogue depends in the first place upon the extent to which the different participants take seriously the full reality of their own faiths as sources for the understanding of the totality of experience.

II

If this is the basis upon which the Christian participates in the dialogue, what understanding of other faiths does this imply? Many different answers have been given and are given to this question. Many volumes would be needed to state and examine them. The following is only a sample of answers for the purpose of orientation.

1. Other religions and ideologies are wholly false and the Christian has nothing to learn from them. On this three things may be said.

(a) The sensitive Christian mind, enlightened by Christ, cannot fail to recognize and to rejoice in the abundant spiritual fruits to be seen in the lives of men and women of other faiths. Here we must simply appeal to the witness of Christians in all ages who have lived in friendship with those of other faiths.

(b) In almost all cases where the Bible has been translated into the languages of the non-Christian peoples of the world, the New Testament word *Theos* has been rendered by the name given by the non-Christian peoples to the one whom they worship as the Supreme Being. It is under this name, therefore, that the Christians who now use these languages worship the God and Father of Jesus Christ. The very few exceptions, where translators have sought to evade the issue by simply transliterating the Greek or Hebrew word, only serve to prove the point; for the converts have simply explained the foreign word in the text of their Bibles by using the indigenous name for God. (I owe this piece of information to a conversation with Dr. Eugene Nida.) The name of the God revealed in Jesus Christ can only be known by using those names for God which have been developed within the non-Christian systems of belief and worship. It is therefore impossible to claim that there is a total discontinuity between the two.

(c) John tells us that Jesus is the light that lightens every man. This text does not say anything about other *religions*, but it makes it impossible for the Christian to say that those outside the church are totally devoid of the truth.

2. The non-Christian religions are the work of devils and their similarities to Christianity are the results of demonic cunning. This view is stated by Justin in his *Apology* and is linked by him with the assertion that the Logos speaking through Socrates and others sought to lead men to the light and away from the work of demons — the Logos who was made man in Jesus Christ. A sharp distinction is here drawn between pagan religions (the work of demons) and pagan philosophy (in which the Logos was shedding his light). Two points should be made regarding this view.

(a) It would be wise to recognize an element of truth here: the sphere of religions is the battlefield *par excellence* of the demonic. New converts often surprise missionaries by the horror and fear with which they reject the forms of their old religion — forms which to the secularized Westerner are interesting pieces of folklore and which to the third-generation successors of the first converts may come to be prized as part of national culture. Religion, including the Christian religion, can be the sphere in which evil exhibits a power against which human reason and conscience are powerless. For religion is the sphere in which a man surrenders himself to something greater than himself.

(b) Even the strange idea that the similarities to Christianity in the non-Christian religions are evidences of demonic cunning points to an important truth. It is precisely at points of highest ethical and spiritual achievement that the religions find themselves threatened by, and therefore ranged against, the gospel. It was the guardians of God's revelation who crucified the Son of God. It is the noblest among the Hindus who most emphatically reject the gospel. It is those who say, "We see," who seek to blot out the light (John 9:41).

3. Other religions are a preparation for Christ: the gospel fulfills them.[11] This way of understanding the matter was strong in Protestant missionary circles in the early years of this century and is fully expressed in the volume of the Edinburgh Conference of 1910 on *The Missionary Message.* The non-Christian religions can be seen as preparation for the gospel, either as the "revelation of deep wants of the human spirit" which the gospel satisfies, or as partial insights which are corrected and completed by the gospel.[12] Obviously such a view can be discussed only on the basis of an intimate and detailed knowledge of mankind's religions. There is indeed a vast missionary literature, mainly written in the first half of this century, which studies the religions from this point of view. Briefly, one has to say that this view had to be abandoned because, in R. Otto's phrase, the dif-

---

11. Perhaps the best-known example is J. N. Farquhar, *The Crown of Hinduism* (Madras: Oxford Univ. Press, 1915).

12. *The Missionary Message* (New York: Revell, 1910), p. 247.

ferent religions turn on different axes. The questions Hinduism asks and answers are not the questions with which the gospel is primarily concerned. One does not truly understand any of the religions by seeing it as a preparation for Christianity. Rather, each religion must be understood on its own terms and along the line of its own central axis.

4. A distinct but related view of the matter, the one dominant at the Jerusalem Conference of 1928, seeks "values" in the religions and claims that while many values are indeed to be found in them, it is only in Christianity that all values are found in their proper balance and relationship. The final statement of the council lists such spiritual values — "the sense of the Majesty of God" in Islam, "the deep sympathy for the world's sorrow" in Buddhism, the "desire for contact with ultimate reality" in Hinduism, "the belief in a moral order of the universe" in Confucianism, and "disinterested pursuit of truth and of human welfare" in secular civilization — as "part of the one Truth."[13] And yet, as the same statement goes on to say, Christ is not merely the continuation of human traditions: coming to him involves the surrender of the most precious traditions. The "values" of the religions do not together add up to him who alone is the truth.

5. A different picture of the relation between Christianity and the other religions is given in the papal encyclical *Ecclesiam Suam* (1964).[14] Here the world religions are seen as concentric circles having the Roman Catholic church at the center and other Christians, Jews, Muslims, other theists, other religionists, and atheists at progressively greater distances. In respect of this proposal one must repeat that the religions cannot be rightly understood by looking at them in terms of their distance from Christianity. They must be understood, so to speak, from within, on their own terms. And one must add that this model particularly fails to do justice to the paradoxical fact central to the whole issue that it is precisely those who are

---

13. Jerusalem Report I, p. 491.
14. See chapter III, "The Dialogue."

in one sense closest to the truth who are in another sense the bitterest opponents of the gospel. Shall we say that the priest and the Levite, guardians of God's true revelation, are nearer to the center than the semipagan Samaritan?

6. Recent Roman Catholic writing affirms that the non-Christian religions are the means through which God's saving will reaches those who have not yet been reached by the gospel. Karl Rahner argues as follows: God purposes the salvation of all men. Therefore he communicates himself by grace to all men, "and these influences can be presumed to be accepted in spite of the sinful state of men." Since a saving religion must necessarily be social, it follows that the non-Christian religions have a positive salvific significance. In this respect they are parallel to the Judaism of the Old Testament, which, though it was a mixture of truth and error, was until the coming of Christ "the lawful religion willed by God for them." The adherent of a non-Christian religion is thus regarded as an anonymous Christian. But a Christian who is explicitly so, "has a much greater chance of salvation than someone who is merely an anonymous Christian."[15]

This scheme is vulnerable at many points. The devout adherent of another religion will rightly say that to call him an anonymous Christian is to fail to take his faith seriously. The argument from the universal saving purpose of God to the salvific efficiency of non-Christian religions assumes, without proving, that it is religion among all the activities of the human spirit which is the sphere of God's saving action. The unique revelation to Jesus Christ of the Old Testament is not adequately recognized.

Its most serious weakness, however, is one which is shared in some degree by the other views we have examined: it assumes that our position as Christians entitles us to know and declare what is God's final judgment upon other people. On the question of the ultimate salvation of those who have never heard the gospel, most contem-

---

15. Karl Rahner, *Theological Investigations* (London: Darton, Longman & Todd, 1966), vol. 5, pp. 115-134.

porary Protestant writers are content to say that it is a matter to be left to the wise mercy of God. Some contemporary Roman Catholics (Hans Küng, for example) rebuke the attitude as a failure to do one's theological duty. Küng even uses the word "supercilious" to characterize this unwillingness to announce in advance the outcome of Judgment Day.[16] I must confess, on the other hand, that I find it astonishing that a theologian should think he has the authority to inform us in advance who is going to be "saved" on the last day. It is not accidental that these ecclesiastical announcements are always moralistic in tone: it is the "men of good will," the "sincere" followers of other religions, the "observers of the law" who are informed in advance that their seats in heaven are securely booked. This is the exact opposite of the teaching of the New Testament. Here emphasis is always on surprise. It is the sinners who will be welcomed and those who were confident that their place was secure who will find themselves outside. God will shock the righteous by his limitless generosity and by his tremendous severity. The ragged beggars from the lanes and ditches will be in the festal hall, and the man who thought his own clothes were good enough will find himself thrown out (Matt. 22:1–14). The honest, hard-working lad will be out in the dark while the young scoundrel is having a party in his father's house (Luke 15). The branch that was part of the vine will be cut off and burned (John 15). There will be astonishment both among the saved and among the lost (Matt. 25:31–46). And so we are warned to judge nothing before the time (I Cor. 4:1–5). To refuse to answer the question which our Lord himself refused to answer (Luke 13:23–30) is not "supercilious"; it is simply honest.

This is not a small matter. It determines the way in which we approach the man of another faith. It is almost impossible for me to enter into simple, honest, open, and friendly communication with another person as long as I have at the back of my mind the feeling that I am one of the saved and he is one of the lost. Such a gulf is too vast to be

---

16. Küng, *On Being a Christian*, p. 99.

bridged by any ordinary human communication. But the problem is not really solved if I decide from my side of the abyss that he also is saved. In either case the assumption is that I have access to the secret of his ultimate destiny. If I were a Hindu, I do not think that even a decision by an ecumenical Christian council that good Hindus can be saved would enable me to join in ordinary human conversation with a Christian about our ultimate beliefs. All such pronouncements go beyond our authority and destroy the possibility of a real meeting. The truth is that my meeting with a person of another religion is on a much humbler basis. I do not claim to know in advance his ultimate destiny. I meet him simply as a witness, as one who has been laid hold of by Another and placed in a position where I can only point to Jesus as the one who can make sense of the whole human situation which my partner and I share as fellow human beings. This is the basis of our meeting.

III

How, from this starting point, do I begin to understand the religion of my partner?

1. Believing that in Jesus God himself is present in the fullness of his being, I am committed to believing that every part of the created world and every human being are already related to Jesus. John expressed this by saying that Jesus is the Word through whom all things came to be, that he is the life of all that is, and that he is the light that gives light to every man. To say this is to affirm that the presence and work of Jesus are not confined within the area where he is acknowledged. John also says, in the same breath, that the light shines in the darkness and that the darkness has not mastered it. His whole Gospel is the elucidation of that statement in terms of actual history. This is not a sort of Christ-monism: there is light and there is darkness. But light shines on the darkness to the uttermost; there is no point at which light stops and darkness begins, unless the light has been put under a bushel. When the light shines

freely one cannot draw a line and say, "Here light stops and darkness begins." But one can and must say, "*There* is where the light shines; go towards it and your path will be clear; turn your back on it and you will go into deeper darkness." One can and must do what John the Baptist did; one can and must "bear witness to the light."

The Christian confession of Jesus as Lord does not involve any attempt to deny the reality of the work of God in the lives and thoughts and prayers of men and women outside the Christian church. On the contrary, it ought to involve an eager expectation of, a looking for, and a rejoicing in the evidence of that work. There is something deeply wrong when Christians imagine that loyalty to Jesus requires them to belittle the manifest presence of the light in the lives of men and women who do not acknowledge him, to seek out points of weakness, to ferret out hidden sins and deceptions as a means of commending the gospel. If we love the light and walk in the light we will also rejoice in the light wherever we find it — even the smallest gleams of it in the surrounding darkness.

Here I am thinking, let it be clearly understood, not only of the evidences of light in the religious life of non-Christians, the steadfastness and costliness of the devotion which so often puts Christians to shame; I am thinking also of the no less manifest evidences of the shining of the light in the lives of atheists, humanists, Marxists, and others who have explicitly rejected the message and the fellowship of the church. "The light" is not to be identified with the religious life of men; religion is in fact too often the sphere of darkness, Christian religion not excluded. The parable of the Good Samaritan is a sharp and constantly needed reminder to the godly of all faiths that the boundary between religion and its absence is by no means to be construed as the boundary between light and darkness.

Christians then, in their dealing with men and women who do not acknowledge Jesus as Lord, will meet them and share with them in a common life, not as strangers but as those who live by the same life-giving Word, and in whom the same life-giving light shines. They will recognize and rejoice in the evidences they find of a response to the same God from whom alone life and light come. They will join with their non-Christian neighbors in all that serves life against death and light against darkness. They will expect to learn as well as to teach, to receive as well as to give, in this common human enterprise of living and building up a common life. They will not be eager to have their particular contributions to the common human task separately labeled as "Christian." They will be happy only if what they do can serve the reign and righteousness of the Father of Jesus who loves all, gives life to all, and purposes the blessing of all.

2. But having said this, having joyfully and gratefully acknowledged all the goodness to be found in every part of the whole human family, it is necessary to go on to say that there is a dark side to this bright picture. The most dark and terrible thing about human nature is our capacity to take the good gifts of God and make them into an instrument to cut ourselves off from God, to establish our independence from God. All the impulses towards good, all the experiences of God's grace, and all the patterns of conduct and of piety which grow from these, can be and have constantly been made the basis for a claim on our own behalf, a claim that we have, so to speak, a standing in our own right. And so, in the name of all that is best in the moral and spiritual experience of the race, we cut ourselves off from the life which God intends for us — a life of pure and childlike confidence in the superabundant kindness of God. This is the tragic story which was enacted in the ministry of Jesus, when — in the name of all that was best and highest in the law and piety of the time — the incarnate Lord was rejected and condemned to death. This is the story which Paul repeats in many different ways, and above all in three chapters (9–11) of the letter to the Romans. It is the story which has been constantly repeated in the history of the church when Christians believe they have, in virtue of their faith and baptism, a claim upon God which others do not have and when they refuse to accept the plain meaning of the teaching of the

apostle that there is no distinction between Christian and pagan because the same Lord is Lord of all and bestows his riches upon all who call upon him (Rom. 10:12).

The cross of Jesus is on the one hand the exposure of this terrible fact and, on the other hand, God's way of meeting it. For, as Paul teaches in many places, while at the cross our human righteousness and piety found themselves ranged in murderous enmity against the God whom they proposed to honor, in that same deed we were offered another kind of righteousness — the righteousness which is God's gift, the relationship of total reconciliation with God present in his own person in the one who is condemned and crucified by our righteousness. This unique historic deed, which we confess as the true turning point of universal history, stands throughout history as witness against all the claims of religion — including the Christian religion — to be the means of salvation. Contrary to much of the teaching we have reviewed, we have to insist that religion is *not* the means of salvation. The message of Jesus, of the unique incarnate Lord crucified by the powers of law, morals, and piety and raised to the throne of cosmic authority, confronts the claim of every religion with a radical negation. We cannot escape this. Jesus comes to the representatives of the highest in human spirituality, as he came to Saul of Tarsus, as one who threatens the most sacred ground on which they stand. He appears as the saboteur, the subverter of the law. It is only after his unconditional claim has been accepted that a man in Christ, like Paul the apostle, can look back and see that Christ has not destroyed the law but fulfilled it.

The experience of Paul is mirrored in that of many converts from Hindu and Muslim faith with whom I have discussed this matter. At the point of crisis Jesus appeared to them as one who threatened all that was most sacred to them. In the light of their experience of life in Christ they now look back and see that he has safeguarded and fulfilled it. To put the matter in another way: the revelation of God's saving love and power in Jesus entitles and requires me to believe that God purposes the salvation of all men, but it does not entitle me to believe that this purpose is to be accomplished in any way which ignores or bypasses the historic event by which it was in fact revealed and effected.

3. The accomplishment of this saving purpose is to be by way of and through a real history — a history whose center is defined by the events which took place "under Pontius Pilate." The end envisaged is the reconciliation of all things in heaven and earth in Christ (Col. 1:20), the "summing up of all things in Christ" (Eph. 1:10), the liberation of the entire creation from its bondage (Rom. 8:19-21). The object to which God's purpose of grace is directed is the whole creation and the whole human family, not human souls conceived as billions of separate monads each detached from its place in the whole fabric of the human and natural world. To think in this way and then to engage in speculations about which of these monads will finally reach the goal and which will not is to distort the biblical picture out of all recognition. The salvation which is promised in Christ and of which his bodily resurrection is the firstfruit, is not to be conceived simply as the fulfillment of the personal spiritual history of each individual human being. To speak in this way is to depart both from Scripture and from a true understanding of what it is to be a person. We are fully persons only with and through others, and in Christ we know that our personal history is so rooted in Christ that there can be no final salvation for each of us until he has "seen of the travail of his soul" and is satisfied (Isa. 53:11). The New Testament itself suggests at many points the need for the patience this requires (Heb. 11:39-40; Rev. 6:9-11). The logic which leads the writer to the Hebrews to say of the saints of former days that "apart from us they should not be made perfect" surely did not cease to operate with the first century. We must equally say that we, and all who are called to the service of God's universal promise of blessing, cannot be made perfect, cannot be saved apart from all who have not yet had the opportunity to respond to the promise. This is the theological context, surely, in which we should try to understand the place in God's purpose of all those millions

who have lived and died out of reach of the story which we believe to be the clue to universal history.

4. Because this salvation is a real consummation of universal history and not simply the separate consummation of individual personal lives conceived as abstracted from the public life of which they are a part, it follows that an essential part of the history of salvation is the history of the bringing into obedience to Christ of the rich multiplicity of ethical, cultural, and spiritual treasures which God has lavished upon mankind. The way in which this is to be understood is shown in the well-known verses from the fourth Gospel.

> I have yet many things to say to you, but you cannot bear them now. When the Spirit of truth comes, he will guide you into all the truth; for he will not speak on his own authority, but whatever he hears he will speak, and he will declare to you the things that are to come. He will glorify me, for he will take what is mine and declare it to you. All that the Father has is mine; therefore I said that he will take what is mine and declare it to you. (John 16:12–15)

We can spell out what is said here in a threefold form.

(a) What can be given to and grasped by this group of first-century Jews is limited by the time and place and circumstances of their lives. It is true knowledge of the only true God and in that sense it is the full revelation of God (John 17:3, 6). But it is not yet the fullness of all that is to be manifested.

(b) It will be the work of the Holy Spirit to lead this little community, limited as it now is within the narrow confines of a single time and place and culture, into "the truth as a whole" and specifically into an understanding of "the things that are to come" — the world history that is still to be enacted.

(c) This does not mean, however, that they will be led beyond or away from Jesus. Jesus is the Word made flesh, the Word by which all that is came to be, and is sustained in being. Consequently all the gifts which the Father has lavished on mankind belong in fact to Jesus, and it will be the work of the Spirit to restore them to their true owner. All these gifts will be truly received and understood when the Holy Spirit takes them and declares their true meaning and use to the church.

We have here the outline of the way in which we are to understand the witness of the church in relation to all the gifts which God has bestowed upon mankind. It does not suggest that the church go into the world as the body with nothing to receive and everything to give. Quite the contrary: the church has yet much to learn. This passage suggests a trinitarian model which will guide our thinking as we proceed. The Father is the giver of all things. They all belong rightly to the Son. It will be the work of the Spirit to guide the church through the course of history into the truth as a whole by taking all God's manifold gifts given to all mankind and declaring their true meaning to the church as that which belongs to the Son. The end to which it all looks is "a plan for the fulness of time, to unite all things to him, things in heaven and things on earth" (Eph. 1:10). The apostle, looking at the marvelous events by which the Gentiles who were outside of the covenant have been brought into it and made members of the household of God, can see in them the signs of the accomplishment of this purpose. As we, from a longer experience of the church's mission to all the nations, look back upon the story of the church and trace its encounter first with the rich culture of the Hellenic world and then with one after another of the cultures of mankind, we can see, with many distractions and perversions and misunderstandings, the beginnings of the fulfillment of this promise.

5. The church, therefore, as it is *in via,* does not face the world as the exclusive possessor of salvation, nor as the fullness of what others have in part, the answer to the questions they ask, or the open revelation of what they are anonymously. The church faces the world, rather, as *arrabōn* of that salvation — as sign, firstfruit, token, witness of that salvation which God purposes for the whole. It can do so only because it lives by the Word and sacraments of the

gospel by which it is again and again brought to judgment at the foot of the cross. And the bearer of that judgment may well be and often is a man or woman of another faith (cf. Luke 11:31–32). The church is in the world as the place where Jesus, on whom all the fullness of the godhead dwells, is present, but it is not itself that fullness. It is the place where the filling is taking place (Eph. 1:23). It must therefore live always in dialogue with the world, bearing its witness to Christ but always in such a way that it is open to receive the riches of God which belong properly to Christ but have to be brought to him. This dialogue, this life of continuous exchange with the world, means that the church itself is changing. It must change if "all that the Father has" is to be given to it as Christ's own possession (John 16:14–15). It does change. Very obviously the church of the Hellenic world in the fourth century was different from the church which met in the upper room in Jerusalem. It will continue to change as it meets ever new cultures and lives in faithful dialogue with them.

6. One may sum up — or at least indicate the direction of — this part of the argument by means of a picture. We have looked at and rejected a series of models which could be expressed in pictures. We will suggest (following Walter Freytag) a simple sketch which may serve to indicate the true basis for dialogue between Christians and those of other faiths.[17] It will be something like this:

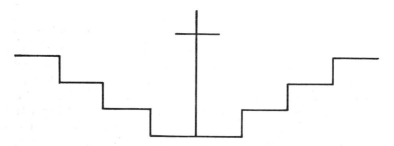

---

17. Walter Freytag, *The Gospel and the Religions* (London: SCM Press, 1957), p. 21.

The staircases represent the many ways by which man learns to rise up towards the fulfillment of God's purpose. They include all the ethical and religious achievements which so richly adorn the cultures of humankind. But in the middle of them is placed a symbol which represents something of a different kind — a historic deed in which God exposed himself in a total vulnerability to all our purposes and in that meeting exposed us as the beloved of God who are, even in our highest religion, the enemies of God. The picture expresses the central paradox of the human situation, that God comes to meet us at the bottom of our stairways, not at the top; that our real ascent towards God's will for us takes us further away from the place where he actually meets us. "I came to call not the righteous, but sinners." Our meeting, therefore, with those of other faiths, takes place at the bottom of the stairway, not at the top. "Christianity" as it develops in history takes on the form of one of those stairways. The Christian also has to come down to the bottom of his stairway to meet the man of another faith. There has to be a *kenosis*, a "self-emptying." The Christian does not meet his partner in dialogue as one who possesses the truth and the holiness of God but as one who bears witness to a truth and holiness which are God's judgment on him and who is ready to hear the judgment spoken through the lips and life of his partner of another faith.

IV

On the basis which has been laid down one can speak briefly of the purpose with which the Christian enters into dialogue with people of other faiths. This purpose can only be obedient witness to Jesus Christ. Any other purpose, any goal which subordinates the honor of Jesus Christ to some purpose derived from another source, is impossible for the Christian. To accept such another purpose would involve a denial of the total lordship of Jesus Christ. A Christian cannot try to evade the accusation that, for him, dialogue is part of his obedient witness to Jesus Christ.

But this does not mean that the purpose of dialogue is to persuade the non-Christian partner to accept the Christianity of the Christian partner. Its purpose is not that Christianity should acquire one more recruit. On the contrary, *obedient* witness to Christ means that whenever we come with another person (Christian or not) into the presence of the cross, we are prepared to receive judgment and correction, to find that our Christianity hides within its appearance of obedience the reality of disobedience. Each meeting with a non-Christian partner in dialogue therefore puts my own Christianity at risk.

The classic biblical example of this is the meeting of Peter with the Gentile Cornelius at Caesarea. We often speak of this as the conversion of Cornelius, but it was equally the conversion of Peter. In that encounter the Holy Spirit shattered Peter's own deeply cherished image of himself as an obedient member of the household of God. ("No, Lord; for I have never eaten anything that is common or unclean.") It is true that Cornelius was converted, but it is also true that "Christianity" was changed. One decisive step was taken on the long road from the incarnation of the Word of God as a Jew of first-century Palestine to the summing up of *all things* in him.

The purpose of dialogue for the Christian is obedient witness to Jesus Christ, who is not the property of the church but the Lord of the church and of all men and who is glorified as the living Holy Spirit takes all that the Father has given to man — all men of every creed and culture — and declares it to the church as that which belongs to Christ as Lord. In this encounter the church is changed, the world is changed, and Christ is glorified.

V

What is to be said, on the basis of the preceding discussion, of the *manner* of interfaith dialogue? We have already suggested that it is the doctrine of the Trinity which provides us with the true grammar of dialogue, and we shall proceed accordingly.

1. We participate in dialogue with men of other faiths believing that we and they share a common nature as those who have been created by the one God who is the Father of all, that we live by his kindness, that we all are responsible to him, and that he purposes the same blessing for us all. We meet as children of one Father, regardless of whether or not our partners have accepted their sonship. This has at least three implications.

(a) We are eager to receive from our partners what God has given them, to hear what God has shown them. In Karl Barth's words, we must have ears to hear the voice of the Good Shepherd in the world at large.

Eagerness to listen, to learn, to receive even what is new and strange will be the mark of one who knows the word of Jesus: "All that the Father has is mine." In our meeting with men of other faiths we are learning to share in our common patrimony as human beings made by the one God in his own image.

(b) We meet in a shared context of things, of nonpersonal entities. The importance of this becomes clear if one recalls the distortion which arises when dialogue is conceived as the encounter of pure naked spirits. For those who regard the mystical experience of undifferentiated unity with pure Being as the core of religion, it will be natural to conceive dialogue as being directed towards a meeting of persons at a level "deeper" than that which can be conceptualized. But, while fully acknowledging that there may be in such a personal meeting more than either of the partners can put into words, it must be insisted that truly personal relationships develop in the context of impersonal realities. We do not become more fully persons by trying to abstract ourselves from the world of things. The Christian in dialogue with men of other faiths rejoices to share with his partners the one common world which is the gift to both from the one God.

(c) Moreover, in the dialogue we meet at a particular place in time in the ongoing history of the world, a history which we believe to be under the providence and rule of God. We meet, not as academics studying dead traditions from the past, but as men and women of faith struggling to meet the demands and opportunities of *this* moment in the life of our city, our nation, our world. To recognize this will prevent us from simply shooting at each other from old fortresses. We shall meet in the open country where all of us, of whatever faith, are being called upon to bring our faith to the test of decision and action in new and often unprecedented situations. It is in this open encounter in the field of contemporary decision that true dialogue takes place. This dialogue may, and often should, lead into common action on many matters of public life.

2. We participate in the dialogue as members in the body of Christ — that body which is sent into the world by the Father to continue the mission of Jesus. This has three consequences for the manner of the dialogue.

(a) It means that we are vulnerable. We are exposed to temptation. We have no defenses of our own. We do not possess the truth in an unassailable form. A real meeting with a partner of another faith must mean being so open to him that his way of looking at the world becomes a real possibility for us. One has not really heard the message of one of the great religions that have moved millions of people for centuries if one has not been really moved by it, if one has not felt in one's soul the power of it. Jesus was exposed to all the power of men's religious and ideological passion, to the point where he could cry, "My God, my God, why did you forsake me?" and yet remain wholly bound to his Father and commit his spirit into his Father's hands. The true disciple will be exposed without defense in his dialogue with men of other faiths and yet will remain bound to Jesus.

(b) One may put this point in the form of the model sketched on page 204. The Christian has to come down to the bottom of the stairway to meet his partner. Much of his "Christianity" may have to be left behind in this meeting.

Much of the intellectual construction, the piety, the practice in which his discipleship of Christ has been expressed may have to be called in question. The meeting place is at the cross, at the place where he bears witness to Jesus as the Judge and Savior both of him and of his partner. In commenting on this approach to dialogue Hick writes:

> This is, I think, a very fruitful approach. But where it will lead must depend to an important extent upon investigations concerning the historical Jesus, to whom it appeals, and of the ways in which the Christian interpretation of him has been formed over the centuries. The all-important question concerns the extent to which the man Jesus is to be understood in terms of the developed theology of the Church.[18]

He goes on to suggest that, if this approach is followed, many of the doctrines which have traditionally been regarded as central to Christianity — the doctrine of the Trinity and of the incarnation, for example — may have to be abandoned.

The issue which is raised here has been discussed in my previous chapter. I have tried to sketch the three-cornered pattern of relationships within which the church has to see to formulate, in its passage from generation to generation and from culture to culture, its answer to the question of who Jesus is. It has to be formulated in openness to the whole testimony of the universal church, in dialogue with the cultures of mankind, and in faithfulness to the tradition as primarily embodied in Scripture. The dialogue with people of other religions will certainly lead to reconsideration and reformulation of Christian doctrines formulated in other circumstances. The possible limits of such reformulation cannot be laid down theoretically in advance. But my whole discussion presupposes the confessional stance; the participants are those for whom Jesus Christ is determinative. Hick explicitly repudiates this stance and adopts that of the modern scientific world view which replaced the "dogmatic slumbers" of Christendom two hundred years

---

18. Hick, "Christian Theology and Inter-Religious Dialogue," p. 8.

ago. From this stance (which is, of course, also a "confessional" stance) the answer to the question "Who is Jesus?" will certainly be very different from any of the traditional Christian formulations. Hick's own writings are ample evidence of this.

The Christian partner in the dialogue of the religions will certainly put his "Christianity" at risk. He must be ready to face the possibility of radical reconsideration of long-accepted formulations. But he does so within his ultimate commitment to Jesus Christ as finally determinative of his way of understanding and responding to all experience.

(c) It follows from this that the Christian will share in the dialogue of the religions as one who is deeply rooted in the life of the church — its worship, teaching, sacraments, and shared discipleship. It is as a member in the body of Christ that he accepts the vulnerability that is a precondition of real encounter. He does not go in his own strength. The world of the religions is the world of the demonic. It is only by being deeply rooted in Christ that one can enter with complete self-emptying and with complete exposure into this world in order to bear faithful witness to Christ.

3. We participate in the dialogue believing and expecting that the Holy Spirit can and will use this dialogue to do his own sovereign work, to glorify Jesus by converting to him both the partners in the dialogue.

(a) The Christian partner must recognize that the result of the dialogue may be a profound change in himself. We have referred to the story of the meeting of Peter and Cornelius, which is the story of radical conversion both for the apostle and for the pagan Roman soldier. Klaus Klostermeier writes as follows of his experience of dialogue with Hindus: "Never did I feel more inadequate, shattered and helpless before God. ... All of a sudden the need for a *metanoia* in depth became irrepressibly urgent."[19] The Holy Spirit who convicts the world of sin, of righteousness, and of

---

19. Klaus Klostermeier, in *Inter-religious Dialogue*, ed. H. Jai Singh (Bangalore, 1967).

judgment may use the non-Christian partner in dialogue to convict the church. Dialogue means exposure to the shattering and upbuilding power of God the Spirit.

(b) The Christian will also believe and expect that the Holy Spirit can use the dialogue as the occasion for the conversion of his partner to faith in Jesus. To exclude this belief and expectation is to reduce dialogue to something much less than its proper importance. What we have said about the "conversion of Peter" in the encounter at Caesarea must not be used to overshadow the conversion of Cornelius, without which there would have been no conversion of Peter. A distinguished Hindu writer on religious and philosophical questions, Dr. R. Sundarara Rajan of Madras, has recently commented on the current developments in the field of Hindu-Christian dialogue. He points out that the emphasis upon a self-critical attitude, the demand that each party should try to see things from within the mind of the other, and the disavowal of any attempt by either side to question the faith of the others can easily mean that dialogue is simply an exercise in the mutual confirmation of different beliefs with all the really critical questions excluded. "If it is impossible to lose one's faith as a result of an encounter with another faith, then I feel that the dialogue has been made safe from all possible risks."[20] A dialogue which is safe from all possible risks is no true dialogue. The Christian will go into dialogue believing that the sovereign power of the Spirit can use the occasion for the radical conversion of his partner as well as of himself.

(c) When we speak of the Holy Spirit we are speaking of the one who glorifies Christ by taking all the gifts of God and showing them to the church as the treasury of Christ (John 16:14–15). The work of the Spirit is the confession of Christ (I John 4:2–3; I Cor. 12:3). The Spirit is not in the possession of the church but is Lord over the church, guiding the church from its limited, partial, and distorted un-

---

20. R. Sundarara Rajan, "Negations: An Article on Dialogue among Religions," *Religion and Society* 21, no. 4, p. 74.

derstanding and embodiment of the truth into the fullness
of the truth in Jesus who is the one in whom all things
consist (Col. 1:17). Not every spirit is the Holy Spirit. Not
every form of vitality is his work. There is need for the gift
of discernment. Peter at Caesarea, and later the congregation in Jerusalem, had need of this discernment to recognize
that this strange and (at first) shocking reversal of deeply
held religious beliefs was the work of the Holy Spirit and
not of the Antichrist (Acts 11:1–18).

There is no substitute for the gift of discernment, no set
of rules or institutional provisions by which we can be
relieved of the responsibility for discernment. Dialogue
cannot be "made safe from all possible risks." The Christian
who enters into dialogue with people of other faiths and
ideologies is accepting the risk. But to put *my* Christianity
at risk is precisely the way by which I can confess Jesus
Christ as Lord — Lord over all worlds and Lord over my
faith. It is only as the church accepts the risk that the
promise is fulfilled that the Holy Spirit will take all the
treasures of Christ, scattered by the Father's bounty over all
the peoples and cultures of mankind, and declare them to
the church as the possession of Jesus.

VI

One of the most common metaphors used in the New Testament to describe the relation of the church to the gospel is
that of stewardship. The church, and especially those called
to any kind of leadership in the church, are servants entrusted with that which is not their property but is the
property of their Lord. That which is entrusted is something of infinite worth as compared with the low estate of
the servants in whose hands it is placed. They are but mud
pots; but that which is entrusted to them is the supreme
treasure (II Cor. 4:7). The treasure is nothing less than "the
mysteries of God" (I Cor. 4:1), "the mystery of the gospel"
(Eph. 6:19), "the mystery which was kept secret for long
ages but is now disclosed and . . . made known to all nations

... to bring about the obedience of faith" (Rom. 16:25-26). It is "the mystery of his will ... to unite all things in him" (Eph. 1:9-10). It is the open secret of God's purpose, through Christ, to bring all things to their true end in the glory of the triune God. It is open in that it is announced in the gospel which is preached to all the nations; it is a secret in that it is manifest only to the eyes of faith. It is entrusted to those whom God has given the gift of faith by which the weakness and foolishness of the cross is known as the power and wisdom of God. It is entrusted to them not for themselves but for all the nations. It is Christ in them, the hope of glory.

A steward can fall into several kinds of temptation. All of them are illustrated in the history of the church and in the parables of Jesus. He can forget that he is only the steward and imagine that he is the proprietor. When this happens the church supposes itself to be the saved while the nations ("the heathen") are the lost. Or he can be lazy, drowsy, and slack, and so allow the treasure to be stolen. When this happens the church falls into a worldly slumber and the world is left without the sound of the gospel. Or the steward may forget the purpose for which the treasure was entrusted to him and keep it wrapped up or buried in the ground. It is to such an unprofitable servant that the master in Jesus' parable says: "You wicked and slothful servant. . . . You ought to have invested my money with the bankers, and at my coming I should have received what was my own with interest" (Matt. 25:14-30). To invest the money with a view to a high rate of interest is to risk the capital. The church has often been afraid to do this, thinking that the faith once delivered to the saints is to be preserved inviolate and without the change of a comma. Verbal orthodoxy then becomes the supreme virtue and syncretism becomes the most feared enemy. When this is the mood real dialogue becomes impossible. And so does real mission. If such a church is strong there can be a kind of proselytism, but there is not that kind of mission which seriously expects the Holy Spirit to take what belongs to Christ and show it to the church, thus leading the church into new truth. The mystery of the gospel is not entrusted to the church to be buried in the ground. It is entrusted to the church in order to be risked in the change and interchange of the spiritual commerce of humanity. It belongs not to the church but to the one who is both head of the church and head of the cosmos. It is within his power and grace to bring to its full completion that long-hidden purpose, the secret of which has been entrusted to the church in order that it may become the open manifestation of the truth to all the nations.